Prayer Is the Key To Unlocking the Unlimited

Larry Rice

New Life Evangelistic Center

Contents

Chapter 1

Prayer is an Opportunity to Get to Know God Better

The greatest moments in my day are those when I walk and talk with God. In the morning as the sun comes up, I can join the birds as they begin their day praising God. As I do this, the rabbits will frequently come out and join us in just being in the presence of God. Their silence reminds me that prayer can also involve just meditating on the goodness of God in the quietness of the morning. Prayer provides such a tremendous opportunity for me to get to know God better.

Walking and talking with God later in the day often means moving among the shadows of the trees, admiring each tree, and reflecting on the fact that God has provided for these trees year after year. Psalm 91:1, 2 says, "He who dwells in the shelter of the Most High will rest in the shadow of the Almighty. I will say of the Lord, 'He is my refuge and my fortress, my God, in whom I trust.'"

Being my refuge and fortress involves those times when my Heavenly Father has said wait, or even no to my prayer request. Frequently that answer is a yes, but at those times when it is a no, I can be assured that my Father in Heaven will provide what is best for me. If I had received a yes for some of those things I asked for, I could

1

have gotten into a lot of trouble. As I get older and look back on life, I find myself thanking Him as much for the waits and nos as I do the yeses.

Daily prayer becomes more and more an opportunity for me to get to know my Father in Heaven better. It opens to me not only the wonders of creation, but the power and the words of the Scriptures. It is there I learn of the great love He has shown me by sending His Son, Jesus, into the world to die for my sins. As a result of His sacrifice, I have passed from death to life (John 5:24). Now I can come as a redeemed sinner into the presence of my Holy Heavenly Father.

When I pray, I become more and more aware how much I am loved by Jesus (John 15:9), and my Heavenly Father (John 16:27). With this awareness dwelling in me, I can receive what Jesus said in John 14:12- 14 when He said, "Very truly I tell you, whoever believes in me will do the works I have been doing, and they will do even greater things than these, because I am going to the Father. And I will do whatever you ask in my name, so that the Father may be glorified in the Son. You may ask me for anything in my name, and I will do it".

Jesus made it perfectly clear that there is power in prayer. I discover this power as I get on my knees and pray. It is then that I begin to understand what it means to breathe in the life of the Spirit of God by exhaling fear and unbelief. When I do this, I will inhale God's grace and goodness.

As a prayer warrior I am one who speaks, hears, tastes, and smells God's goodness in prayer. I become like the woman who was bleeding in Luke 8:43-48 and touched the very hem of Jesus' garment. This touch involves grasping the impossible, knowing that with God all things are possible. Touching the hem of Jesus' garment also means refusing to believe the lies and accusations of Satan, and instead, receive the promises of Scripture and make them my own.

It is for this reason; I must daily read the Bible in order that I can absorb the promises of God. **As I meditate on these promises and pray, I get to know God better and better.**

When Satan tries to hinder my prayer life through condemnation, I can claim the promise found in Romans 8:1 where it says, "Therefore, there is now no condemnation for those who are in Christ Jesus."

On a recent prayer walk, as the Holy Spirit was showing me the wonders of creation and how God cares for it, I was reminded not to be anxious but instead follow the directives of Phil. 4:6-7, "Do not be anxious about anything, but in every situation, by prayer and petition, with thanksgiving, present your requests to God. And the peace of God, which transcends all understanding, will guard your hearts and your minds in Christ Jesus."

As I enter into prayer with thanksgiving, out of my innermost being rivers of water begin to flow (John 7:38). This water is spiritual oil to my thirsty soul. It provides a peace that passes all understanding (John 14:27).

I am learning that prayer also involves listening. When I am outside praying and hear the wind blowing through the branches of the trees, I am reminded of the ongoing work of the Holy Spirit.

Even in silence I can hear God saying, "Be still and know that I am God" (Psalm 46:10) and declaring in John 14:6, "I am the way, and the truth and the life."

Prayer makes me a better listener when it comes to hearing and responding to the needs of the poor, sick, fatherless, widowed, hurting, and homeless. Psalm 41:1 says, "Blessed is he who has regard for the weak; the Lord delivers him in times of trouble."

As I get to know my Lord better, I become increasingly aware of His love for the mother who must raise her children in a dark, cold house where the utilities are shut off. I must seek God fervently how to help her as well as how I can express His love in word and deed to those who are forced to sleep outside without shelter.

If I am going to have a prayerful relationship with my Heavenly Father through Christ Jesus, I must not be indifferent to the needs of the poor. Proverbs 21:13 says, "Whoever shuts his ears to the cry of the poor will also cry himself and not be heard."

At New Life Evangelistic Center, we have found that direct financial grants for those with urgent needs, gifts of blankets, shelter, food, water, on the job training programs, etc. gives us unprecedented opportunities to share the love of Jesus Christ in both word and deed. I have seen once we have done everything we can for that brother and sister in need we are free to go to God in intercessory prayer saying with a clear conscience, "Father, we have done everything we can in faith with the resources you have given us. Now we ask you in the name of Jesus Christ for your direct divine intervention in this situation." **The result - - IT WORKS! Miracles happen and the need is supplied!**

As a prayer warrior, I am strengthened and empowered daily through the promises of Scripture. Martin Luther, who once said he had so much to do on a certain day that he had to pray for an extra hour, declared, "Our Lord God could not but hear me; I threw the sack down before His door. I rubbed God's ear with all His promises about hearing prayer."

Jesus Himself reminds me that I am to hammer away in prayer until a breakthrough comes (Luke 18:1-8; 11:5-13). I call that a **PUSH** prayer. This spells out **P**raying **U**ntil **S**omething **H**appens.

Prayer challenges me to get to know God better and to take new steps of faith in obedience to His Word. As I move forth by faith, I continue to see my Lord Jesus doing exceedingly more than I can ask or think. As He does this my faith grows because Christ "is able to do exceedingly abundantly above all that we ask or think, according to the power that worketh in us" (Ephesians 3:20 ASV).

There are many verses in the Bible that say that we are to pray with faith knowing that with God all things are possible. These faith building verses from the Bible include:

Matthew 17:20 – "So Jesus said to them, 'For assuredly, I say to you, if you have faith as small as a mustard seed, you will say to this

4

mountain, 'Move from here to there,' and it will move; and nothing will be impossible for you."

Matthew 19:26 – "But Jesus looked at them and said to them, 'With men this is impossible, but with God all things are possible.'"

Mark 11:24 – "Therefore I say to you, whatever things you ask when you pray, believe that you receive them, and you will have them."

Luke 1:37 – "For with God nothing will be impossible."

Philippians 4:13 – "I can do all things through Christ who strengthens me."

As I pray, knowing that with God all things are possible for those who believe, I can experience the victory of Christ over disease, greed, oppression, injustice, and death. When I fix my prayers on the divine possibility available, I can believe God for miracles.

This morning as I was walking and praying the sun rose and a new day dawned. As the birds were singing, I joined them in praise as I thanked God for how He had met a major need in my life.

A rooster was crowing in the distance as I passed under a tree and heard two squirrels arguing. At this hour, the squirrels are usually asleep, but in this case these two were awake and were really going at it. As they shouted at each other I thought of all the families who spend so much time arguing and fighting day after day. I began to pray for these families and those living in the houses I was passing by. I prayed for our city that God would send a revival and His love would flow.

As I walked, I talked with God as Adam and Eve did in the Garden of Eden. I thanked my Heavenly Father for sending Jesus and how His death and resurrection provides salvation and hope for all eternity. Because Jesus paid the price for my sins, I can come into the presence of a Holy Almighty God.

As I pray and believe the promises of the scriptures and grow in my relationship with God through the power of the Holy Spirit, I will know that "All things work together for good, for those who are called according to His purpose" (Romans 8:28).

5

In addition to praying for a greater release of the Holy Spirit, Jesus tells us to pray for a greater measure of justice. "And will not God bring about justice for His chosen ones, who cry out to Him day and night?" (Luke 18:7).

If we will but look, we will see the injustice in the lives of the hurting and homeless all around us. Jesus said, to those who are Christian in name only, and have no concern for justice, "Not everyone who says to me 'Lord, Lord,' shall enter the Kingdom of God, but he who does the will of my Father in heaven" (Matt. 7:21). Jesus shared the will of God when He said, "For I was hungry and you gave me something to eat, I was thirsty and you gave me something to drink, I was a stranger and you invited me in..." (Matthew 25:35).

When we allow the greedy to trample on the rights of the fatherless, widowed, or homeless, we have forgotten the God who made them and called us to pray for justice and defend those that many look down upon.

Experiencing the reality of the Risen Christ in the depths of our very being, gives us the Holy boldness to directly confront the principalities and powers that oppress those in need.

"For we do not wrestle against flesh and blood, but against principalities, against powers, against the rulers of the darkness of this age, against spiritual hosts of wickedness in the heavenly places" (Ephesians 6:12).

The shutdown of 1411 Locust in St. Louis was a direct attack from the pits of hell. Souls were being saved and lives were being changed because of the ministry taking place in that building.

Now in the name of Jesus we must come against these "rulers of the darkness of the age," who are determined to keep the homeless out of sight and out of mind. We do this as we stand on the promises of God's Word and stand steadfast in the name of Jesus, "against spiritual hosts of wickedness in the heavenly places."

Then as we confess our sins unto the Risen Christ, we ask Him to strengthen us "With power through His Spirit in our inner being so

6

that Christ may dwell in our hearts through faith" (Ephesians 3:16-17).

Now we must daily go to God in prayer. Then, we will remain steadfast, immovable, abounding in the work of Jesus Christ. "For we are His workmanship, created in Christ Jesus for good works, which God prepared beforehand that we should walk in them" (Ephesians 2:10).

What a marvelous, Heavenly Father we have. He loves us so much that He sent His only begotten Son to die for our sins. Now, we can talk to Him at any time and in any place as we journey toward eternity.

Our Father in Heaven invites us to pray and get to know Him better. Let us not waste another moment but instead come to God and pray without ceasing as I Thessalonians 5:16-18 tells us to do. "Be joyful always; pray continually; give thanks in all circumstances, for this is God's will for you in Christ Jesus."

Chapter 2

Pray Believing and Watch the Miracles that Will Follow

In Malachi 3:10 God challenges us, **"Test me. Try me. Let me prove it to you."** Jesus tells us in Matthew 7:7, we accept this challenge and, **"Ask and it will be given to you; seek and you will find; knock and the door will be opened to you."**

At a young age accepted the challenge and started asking, seeking, and knocking. Once when I was in my early teens, I went turkey hunting with my father. I sat in a blind all morning alone waiting, waiting, and waiting but no turkey came out. Then I heard the truck coming up the road to get me. At that moment I blurted out in prayer, "Dear God send out one turkey gobbler." No sooner had the prayer been said and out walked one turkey gobbler. I knew that turkey was a direct answer to my prayer.

Years later, while at senior college I was going around a sharp bend on an icy road when suddenly my car skidded out of control. It was about to go off the road into a five foot drop off when I cried out, "Lord save me, and I will read your word daily." At that moment it was like a dozen angels grabbed that car and straightened it, bringing it to a complete stop.

As the years passed and I began to read, meditate, and take God's Word and apply it to the needs I faced daily, I started seeing miracles. Jesus poured out His Holy Spirit upon me and brought forth New Life Evangelistic Center. At New Life we would pray, and God would miraculously provide our food for the next meal along with the funds necessary to pay the bills.

When we would get sick, we would remember that by His stripes we are healed. Yes, we knew that the shed blood of Jesus Christ cleansed us from all of our sins but as we faced sickness and did not have money for doctors or insurance, we had to believe that when Jesus was beaten His stripes also provided healing as it says in Isaiah 53:5.

I remember the time when Chris, my son as a young child, got very sick in the middle of the night. I took him to the emergency room of the hospital. I sat there on that cold night in the waiting room while everyone seemed to cough around us. As I sat there, I began to realize that by taking him to a place surrounded by sick people and waiting for hours for help I might have been doing him more harm than good. Finally, we got up and went home and after praying saw him get better in the next two days. Either way, we knew we had to believe God for a miracle. This miracle would be either a miraculous provision for the doctor bill or a complete healing.

Don't get me wrong I believe doctors are a great gift from God. What I have learned over the years is that first I must pray and then seek the doctors' help under God's direction.

The foundation point for my belief in answered prayers is the historical resurrection of Jesus Christ. It is the reality of this resurrection which changes everything. Because Christ is Risen the miracle of heaven is awaiting us after death. Jesus Christ rose from the dead and now we can rise from the paralysis of unbelief into a realm of being fully persuaded that God answers prayer.

"This is the victory that has overcome the world, even our faith. Who is it that overcomes the world? Only he (and she) who believes that Jesus is the Son of

9

God" (I John 5:4-5). Jesus took my sins and your sins upon Himself on the cross and ultimately conquered death through His physical resurrection. This miracle provides us with the power we need to overcome the world.

As I get older I continue to learn how God is able to answer prayers on a daily basis if we will have faith in Him. If you and I are going to accomplish that which God has called us to do we also must be fully persuaded that God has the power to do what He has promised. We have to believe the words that Paul declared in Ephesians 3:20 when he stated, **"Now to Him who is able to do immeasurably more than we can ask or imagine, according to His power that is at work within us."**

He **"is able to do immeasurably more than we can ask or imagine"**. If we are going to understand this power, we must know what it means to be in Christ Jesus. II Corinthians 5:17 says, **"If anyone is in Christ, he is a new creation; the old has gone, the new has come!"**

This power is a result of repenting of our sins and committing our lives to Jesus and living daily under His direction. When this happens, we are not just reformed, rehabilitated, or reeducated, but we are recreated (a new creation) living in union with Jesus Christ. **"So then, just as you received Christ Jesus as Lord, continue to live in Him, rooted and built up in Him, strengthened in the faith as you were taught, and over-flowing with thankfulness"** (Colossians 2:6-7).

As I continue to live in Christ, rooted and built up in Him I know I can ask my Heavenly Father for anything, and everything to complete the job He has given me to do. For that reason, when He presented the opportunity to build a full power television station in St. Louis, I said yes Lord. I must admit, I didn't have a full under-standing of what was involved in building a TV station, yet I believed in God and His ability to bring forth the miracle of Channel 24.

Even after KNLC Channel 24 was miraculously built and went on the air, the New Life staff continued to face one need after another. We were learning it wasn't enough to just believe in miracles, but we also had to have an overcoming faith where we were fully persuaded to the extent that we would not give up when problems occurred. As I John 5:4 says, **"For whatsoever is born of God overcomes the world: and this is the victory that overcomes the world, even our faith"**. It is this faith which allows us to be fully persuaded that God answers prayer.

We must be constantly reminded that, by being in Christ, we are **"a new creation; the old has gone, the new has come**!" (II Corinthians 5:17). This newness is a result of the miracle of salvation that Jesus has provided. As a saved people we are a victorious people for, "Though we live in the world, we do not wage war as the world does. The weapons we fight with are not the weapons of the world. On the contrary, they have the divine power to demolish strongholds. We demolish arguments and every pretension that sets itself up against the knowledge of God and we take captive every thought to make it obedient to Christ" (II Corinthians 10:3-5).

This obedience to Christ involves responding to the needs of our community. For example, during the 1980 heat crisis and the sever cold of the winter of 1982, the NLEC staff saw God provide the miracles of fans, air conditioners, wood furnaces, heaters, and blankets. As we have continued to pray throughout the years, we have witnessed the miracles God provided for the poor, elderly and homeless in response to prayer.

It was faith which enabled us to believe in miracles. This faith was activated through the Word of God. "Faith comes from hearing the message, and the message is heard through the Word of Christ" (Romans 10:17).

In order for faith to do its perfect work we must move forth daily seeking God's direction and maintaining an attitude of humility. "Do not think of yourself more highly than you ought, but rather think of yourself with sober judgment, in accordance with the measure of faith God has given you. Just as each of us has one body with many members and these members do not all have the same function, so in

Christ we who are many form one body, and each member belongs to all the others. We have different gifts, according to the grace given us" (Romans 12:3-6).

In the context of a community of faith, we are able to overcome the daily pressures by looking to Christ, the hope of glory. **Our faith is not in our faith but in our Living Lord** who reminds us in His Word to "Be devoted to one another in brotherly (and sisterly) love. Honor one another above yourselves. Never be lacking in zeal, but keep your spiritual fervor, serving the Lord. Be joyful in hope, patient in affliction, and faithful in prayer. Share with God's people who are in need. Practice hospitality. Bless those who persecute you; bless and do not curse. Rejoice with those who rejoice; mourn with those who mourn. Live in harmony with one another. Do not be proud but be willing to associate with people of low position. Do not be conceited" (Romans 12:10-16).

Victorious faith which believes God daily to answers prayer involves **reading the Bible, walking humbly with God, and living a life of love** in a community of people who are dedicated to serving **Jesus Christ**. It is in this community of fellow believers that I discover that when I am facing an impossible situation, I can get others to agree with me in prayer. As we pray, we release our faith knowing Jesus can perform the miraculous. In Mark 9, in verse 22, the father of the demon possessed son cries out to Jesus, "If you can do anything, take pity on us and help us." In response, we see Jesus saying, "Everything is possible for him who believes."

As one who believes in the power of prayer I must be fully persuaded "...that in all things God works for the good of those who love Him, who have been called according to His purpose" (Romans 8:28). I must always remember that true prayer comes from the heart where a victory has resulted from an interior battlefield in which Christ now reigns supreme. In such a life, inner liberty results when we are free to act in obedience to God's Word and not the expectations of others. As this happens the Christ reigns supreme and God is free to answer our prayers.

Praying and believing in miracles also involves accepting God's will when He says no to a request and declares, **"Be still and know that I am God"** (Psalm 46:10). We must then hear Him declaring in the midst of our doubts and uncertainties, "**I am the way, and the truth, and the life**" (John 14:6).

When Victor Anderson came as a homeless man to NLEC many years ago, a psychiatrist had told him he was an "incurable alcoholic". While he was at New Life, he gave his life to Jesus Christ and experienced the miracle of Salvation. Then, in the NLEC Community he grew in his faith into a great man of God. When he moved on through death into the eternal arms of Jesus, Vic left a legacy of faith and an example of what it means to serve Christ. It was the word of God that had sustained Vic throughout his battle with cancer and prayer which empowered him.

In the battles I encounter daily, I must never forget to put on the full armor of God as I take up the sword of the Word and the weapon of Prayer (Ephesians 6:10-20). As Walter Wink writes, "When we pray, we are not sending a letter to a celestial White House where it is sorted among piles of others. We are engaging in an act of co-creation, in which one little sector of the universe rises up and becomes translucent, incandescent – a vibratory center of power that radiates the power of the universe."

Daily with each difficulty I encounter, I must pray, drawing my strength from Christ, as I declare along with Paul, **"I can do everything through Him (Jesus) who gives me strength"** (Philippians 4:13).

I can never forget that **"this is the victory that has overcome the world, even our faith. Who is it that overcomes the world? Only he (or she) who believes that Jesus is the Son of God"** (I John 5:4-5).

No matter what circumstances you and I may encounter we must pray and believe that "**we are more than conquerors through Him who loved us**" (Romans 8:37).

Scripture is filled with one promise after another, along with example after example of how God answers prayer. Let Him show you this now by being fully persuaded that, "... **He is able to do exceedingly above what you can even ask or think**" (Ephesians 3:20).

Chapter 3

Prayer Is Listening

P raying is not just talking to God, it is also listening to what God would say to us. Praying is listening every moment day and by night as we pray because God desires to speak to us. The problem is we are so preoccupied with our own thoughts that we shut out God's voice as we pray.

Each day thousands of God's words will descend upon us, only to fall to the ground unheeded because we will not listen. We often do not listen because our daily worries keep us from hearing God's voice as He speaks.

Prayer allows us to get to know our Lord God better. As this happens, Jesus says in John 10:27, "My sheep hear my voice and I know them, and they follow me."

Daily we should be praying "Lord, do you have anything to say to me?" We don't often say that because we really don't want to hear from God since it might interrupt our plans and desires.

One of the reasons that we may be experiencing so much stress in life is the result of deciding what we want to do without first praying and asking God what His will is... Then after earnest prayer when our desires are not fulfilled, we feel God has failed us. We could have saved ourselves considerable stress by first seeking God's direction and then listening for His response. Once receiving such direction, we can then proceed to move forward knowing in our hearts **He is leading us.** When we do that, we will not have to question when obstacles are encountered whether we should keep going because we had already received God's direction as we prayed before we got started.

In order to hear the voice of God and learn what His will is for our lives, we must have the Holy Spirit clean out our spiritual ears. Once we recognize that it is sin that plugs up our spiritual ears, be it pride, greed, lust, or anything else that keeps us from hearing the voice of God we will repent and ask Christ to flush those sins from our lives through His redemptive work on the cross.

The next thing we must do if we want to hear the voice of God is to surrender our will to Him. He is then free to speak to us and lead us into His perfect will using a variety of methods. These include:

[1] **God speaks to us through His Word.** For me, this involves seeking God through prayer and the reading of the Scriptures. Then, I will experience an affirmation in my inner spirit that I am to pursue a certain direction. The reason I must first search the Scriptures is that the Holy Spirit will lead us by wisdom and direction based upon the knowledge and obedience of the Scriptures.

I know from personal experience that when I am in close fellowship with Christ, His Spirit will speak to my Spirit in the areas that I need guidance. This involves a peace that passes all understanding. Paul and Silas are an example of this as they sang while in prison (Acts 16:22-25). Although they were locked up, they knew God was going to do a mighty work through their imprisonment. That mighty work involved the jailer and his whole household being saved.

In the Word of God, we also get specific direction on how to deal with each and every problem in life. This is given through direct commands and the examples of individuals who obeyed God and those who did not. As Psalm 119:15 and 16 says, "I meditate on your precepts and consider your ways. I delight in your decrees; I will not neglect your Word."

[2] **God leads us, as we pray and ask Him to speak to us, through the cries of the poor and homeless.** Instead of listening to these cries for help as we pray and read the scriptures, we shut these cries out as we become preoccupied by our own needs while we pray.

Even in the church many desiring to be blessed do not want someone to stand up in the middle of the worship and cry out, "I am worn out crying for help; my throat is parched. My eyes fail, looking for God. Those who hate me without reason outnumber the hairs of my head; many are my enemies without cause, those who seek to destroy me. I am forced to restore what I did not steal" (Psalm 69:3,4) see also Psalm 102:19, 20).

If we want to know and do the will of God, we must be willing to hear the cries of the suffering. Proverbs 21:13 says, "If a man (that includes a woman also) shuts his ears to the cry of the poor, he too will cry out and not be answered."

God desires to speak to us concerning the issues of injustice. When the cries of the homeless, imprisoned and elderly are no longer heard, God's will for justice and compassion is not fulfilled. As a result, issues of structural violence and injustice get accepted and legitimized.

God's response is, "When you spread out your hands in prayer, I will hide my eyes from you; even if you offer many prayers, I will not listen. Your hands are full of blood; wash and make yourselves clean. Take your evil deeds out of my sight. Stop doing wrong, learn to do right, seek justice, encourage the oppressed. Defend the cause of the fatherless, plead the cause of the widow" (Is. 1:15-17).

It was New Year's Eve Day, December 31st, 2023, that I found myself in Tower Grove Park deeply burdened over what I, along with the other staff were finding among the unsheltered who were living outside. As I prayed, I could hear their cries of desperation for help. For weeks it was in my heart to develop a vision for a city of refuge.

17

At this sanctuary, the homeless would receive food, clothing, shelter, on the job training, mental health, drug, and alcohol treatment, and more under the direction of our Lord, Jesus Christ.

I had been continually giving God my excuses for not developing such a vision. It was then that He reminded me of how in the past when He gave me a vision for a Christian TV Station, I did not have a precise location. That would come later. So, in obedience to the leading of the Spirit and the work of God I proceeded to develop such a vision even though its exact location had not been shown to me.

[3] **The Holy Spirit speaks to us through specific revelations.** An example of this is how the Holy Spirit led Peter in Acts 10:11-23 to go to the home of Cornelius and share the Gospel. Throughout the Scriptures we see example after example about how God directly spoke to those who sought Him. All such revelation must be based on the Word of God. Anything contrary to the Scriptures is not from God.

[4] **God speaks to us through difficult experiences.** The life of Joseph is an example that we find in Genesis 37-50. Joseph, instead of panicking when he was sold into slavery, prayed. As he trusted God every step of the way Joseph ended up as the number two leader in Egypt. When his brothers, who sold him into slavery later met him as the ruler of Egypt, they panicked. In response to their fear Joseph said, "You intended to harm me, but God intended it for good to accomplish what is now being done, the saving of many lives" (Genesis 50:20).

[5] **Closing Various Doors.** God closed the doors to where Jonah was going by having him swallowed by a whale and then put ashore in Nineveh where he was told to preach the Word of God. A second example is that of Balaam whose donkey refused to move forward and spoke to Balaam stopping him from being killed (Numbers 22: 21-31).

We need to tune into God's frequency through prayer and hear

His voice. His frequency is constantly broadcasting. He is there and we do not need to be afraid. We receive this assurance through the reading and hearing of the Scriptures and seeing His love in the wonders of creation. When we are not doing that and praying, we get out of tune with God and cannot hear His voice. Then, we become ungrateful, stressed, frustrated, and anxiety ridden. As we do this, we are not able to recognize and hear the direction Jesus gives us on a daily basis.

Hearing the voice of God involves getting beyond ourselves, reaching out to others, and letting the love of God flow through us as He tells in Matthew 25:40, He says, "I tell you the truth, whatever you did for one of the least of these you did for me."

Being able to hear God's voice to the extent His love can flow through us involves being freed from the prison of self. As David cried out in Psalms 142:7, "Set me free from my prison, that I may praise your name."

Freed from our prison of fear, ungratefulness, and presumption results in hearing God's voice, as He speaks to us through His gift of creation. Psalms 19:1-4 tell us, "The heavens declare the glory of God; the skies proclaim the work of His hands. Day after day they pour forth speech; night after night they reveal knowledge. They have no speech; they use no words; no sound is heard from them. Yet their voice goes out into all the earth, their words to the ends of the world."

In order to hear Christ's voice spoken through creation I want to encourage you to go on a prayer walk in the midst of creation. Take your Bible with you along with an open receptive heart that is willing to listen to the voice of the Lord.

When we pray and listen to God speak as He speaks through His creation, we find ourselves at the heartbeat of life. It is there in the beginning God spoke and life came forth (Genesis 1).

All around us the voice of God can be heard. As you pray and listen, God's voice will calm you and lead you. It will reassure you and enlighten you. The voice of God will not only encourage you and comfort you, but it will convict you of those things that are keeping you from hearing His voice as you pray.

There are so many other voices coming at us day after day. These voices whether they are from Satan, the world, or our own fleshly desires, all keep us from hearing the voice of God. These other voices will confuse and discourage us. They will push and frighten us as they fill us with worry and discouragement.

Now we have a choice. Will we keep listening to all those other voices or will we let God speak to us. The choice is ours. He desperately wants to talk to us but now we must listen.

When we pray things will change, if we will listen to His response. Then hope will arise. He will give peace where there is anxiety and hope where there is hopelessness. Jesus said, "I will give you life and all its fullness" but remember He also said, "My sheep hear my voice and I know them, and they follow me" (John 10:27).

Let us resolve today that we will pray and listen to God's voice and obey Him.

Chapter 4

Prayer In Response to the Groaning of Creation and the Cries of the Hurting

Genesis 21 tells us that when Hagar and her son ran out of hope and water as they wandered in the desert, *"She put the boy under one of the bushes. Then she went off and sat down nearby, about a bowshot away, for she thought, "I cannot watch the boy die.' And as she sat there nearby, she began to sob. God heard the boy crying, and the angel of God called to Hagar from heaven and said to her, 'What is the matter, Hagar? Do not be afraid. God has heard the boy crying as he lies there"* (Verses 15-17)

Why are we as people of God not able to hear the cries of the hurting and the groaning of creation? Because we cannot hear such cries, we are not able to pray with power and be the activists God has called us to be. Paul declared, "We know that the whole creation has been groaning as in the pains of childbirth" (Romans 8:22).

As we study the Scriptures, we see that the Biblical landscape is filled with the cries of the afflicted and the lamentations of the suffering. The Scriptural witness contains loud and sustained outbursts on behalf of the least of these. "You trample on the poor and force them to give you grain... You oppress the righteous and take bribes and you deprive the poor of justice in the courts..." (Amos 5). "The earth dries up and withers, the world languishes and withers, the exalted of the earth languish" (Isaiah 24:4).

"In his arrogance the wicked hunts down the weak, who are caught in the schemes he devises. He boasts of the cravings of his heart; he blesses the greedy and reviles the Lord. In his pride the wicked does not seek him; in all his thoughts there is no room for God. He lies in wait like a lion in cover; he lies in wait to catch the helpless; he catches the helpless and drags them off in his net. His victims are crushed, they collapse; they fall under his strength" (Psalms 10:2-4, 9-10). These include the victimized children many who are homeless or residing in homes with no utilities, senior citizens lacking resources for medication, along with millions of others without adequate health care locked into substandard housing and unemployment or incarcerated without adequate legal defense. The witness of their needs should awaken us to the injustices we must come to terms with.

The question is what happens to the prayer life of a church, or individual for whom the cries of the suffering are excluded? What happens to all of us when we let the cries be silenced and ignored in prisons, on the streets, in the psychiatric wards, old age centers, polluted streams or even holes in the ozone layer? In our society, the groans of creation and human cries for justice are often avoided. The homeless are driven out of the downtown areas, with those making too much noise locked up, labeled mentally ill or heavily medicated. John Grisham in his book, "The Innocent Man" describes how Ada, Oklahoma prosecutors put an innocent man, Ron Williamson, on death row with a case built on junk science and the testimony of jail house snitches. The more Williamson would cry out that he was innocent the more the systems would medicate him in order to silence his cry for justice.

We often feel uncomfortable with the groaning of creation and the cries of the oppressed. Such lamentations tell us everything is not all right, and we must exercise faith to address injustices. The absence of lament in worship eliminates the questions of justice about the things we call blessings which frequently come at the cost of great suffering for others. As a result God declares, "When you come to appear before me, who has asked this of you, this trampling of my courts? Stop bringing meaningless offerings! Your incense is detestable to Me" (Isaiah 1:12-13). "Away with the noise of your songs! I will not listen to the music of your harps. But let justice roll on like a river, righteousness like a never-failing stream" (Amos 5:23-24).

Why are those who claim to be Christians so quick to support policies that make it easier to incarcerate and execute the poor, lock up the migrant, cut Medicaid, and keep the homeless out of sight and out of mind? It was Jesus who said, "As often as you have done it unto the least of these, even so you have done it unto Me."

Have we forgotten that the Christian memorial meal "The Lord's Supper" comes out of the suffering of one who was executed as an innocent man? This sacrament should cause its participants to reach out through the love of Christ to those who are grieving and cast aside. It should cause us to respond to the world's suffering and injustice.

To attend to the cries of the suffering and the groaning of creation's environmental destruction will deepen our prayer life and awaken us to the power of the embodiment of the Kingdom of God. It is these cries that awaken us to the suffering which also causes us to obey our Savior who declared, "The Spirit of the Lord is on me, because He has anointed me to preach good news to the poor. He has sent me to proclaim freedom for the prisoners and recovery of sight for the blind, to release the oppressed to proclaim the year of the Lord's favor" (Luke 4:18-19).

To receive Jesus as Lord and Savior is to receive His calling to pray for the needs of the hurting and the groaning of creation. Then in obedience to Christ we must take direct action in His name in their behalf.

This direct action involves the call to "defend the afflicted among the people and save the children of the needy: he will crush the oppressor" (Psalm 72:4).

At a time when so much legislation is being passed which cuts services for the needy and environmental protection, while tax cuts and tax benefits are being issued to the rich, those in power must be reminded, "He who oppresses the poor to increase his wealth and he who gives gifts to the rich – both come to poverty...Do not exploit the poor because they are poor and do not crush the needy in court, for the Lord will take up their case and will plunder those who plunder them" (Proverbs 22:16, 22-23).

Why is it so easy to support laws which try to silence the cries of the distressed and support the policies that remove those issuing such cries, from our midst? Where are the people of faith who are praying and dare to bring these cries into the boardrooms, the government offices, and the churches? How is it that we have allowed the war on poverty to become the war on the impoverished, which works to marginalize and silence those in need?

Are we praying as innocent people are killed in Israel, Gaza, Ukraine, and other countries around the world? Are we listening as we pray, and God declares, "What have you done? Listen: your brother's blood cries out to me from the ground" (Genesis 4:10).

We must hear the cries of the poor and the groaning of creation, to the extent we will engage in deep prayer that those in authority "will come to the knowledge of the truth" and stop basing their decisions upon the advice of lobbyists and rich political donors.

When Paul urged us to pray for those in authority, it was not a request to bless their acts of injustice but a request for prayer that they might be saved. He states, "I urge, then, first of all, that requests, prayers, intercession, and thanksgiving be made for everyone – and Kings and those in authority, that we might live peaceful and quiet lives in all godliness and holiness. This is good, and pleases God our Savior, who wants all men (and women) to be saved, and to come to a knowledge of the truth" (I Timothy 2:1-4).

Before we can expect the politicians to be delivered from indifference to the cries of the poor and the groaning of creation those who claim to be the people of God must first pray and repent of their indifference. God has declared, "If My people, who are called by My name, will humble themselves and pray and seek My face and turn from their wicked ways, then will I hear from heaven and will forgive their sin and will heal their land" (2 Chronicles 7:14).

The sins of humanity directly contribute to the destruction of creation. "There is no faithfulness, no love, no acknowledgement of God in the land. There is only cursing, lying and murder, stealing and adultery; they break all bonds, and bloodshed follows bloodshed. Because of this the land mourns, and all who live in it waste away; the beasts of the field and the birds of the air and the fish of the sea are dying" (Hosea 4:1-3).

Creation is groaning for humanity to turn from its sins of greed and self-destruction and enter into the glorious freedom that Christ's redemptive work provides. "For the creation was subjected to frustration, not by its own choice, but by the will of the one who subject it, in hope that the creation itself will be liberated from its bondage to decay and brought into the glorious freedom of the children" (Romans 8:20-21).

Today we live in a society that is hostile to the poor and homeless. Rules, regulations, and ordinances are constantly being created that are making it increasingly difficult to house the homeless and feed the hungry. How many future saints have lost their saltiness because the desires of the rich and powerful take more priority in their lives than meeting the needs of the starving and homeless?

At such a time like this we must have our eyes opened and pray and pray some more. As we pray, we must be passionately seeking God's will for our lives. Prayer is the language of the poor. In Psalms 26:1 we read, "Bow down thine ear, O Lord, hear me: for I am poor and needy." Then Psalms 34:6 declares, "This poor man cried, and the Lord heard him."

We must begin to pray, "Lord, I don't want to forget any longer to be the salt of the earth you have called me to be." Jesus said in Luke 14:34-35, "Salt is good for seasoning. But if it loses its flavor, how do you make it salty again? Flavorless salt is good neither for the soil nor for fertilizer. It is thrown away. Anyone who is willing to hear should listen and understand."

The time has come for us to repent of our prayerlessness, indifference, and salt-lessness. As Joel 2:12 declares, "Now, therefore says the Lord. Turn to Me and with all your heart, with fasting, with weeping, and with mourning."

The web of impurity and injustice is tightening around the country. The cup of sin is filling up. The handwriting is on the wall (Daniel 5:26-27). Someone has said that hell is filled with unrepentant sinners who are blind to the needs around them, while heaven is filled with sinners who have repented and can see God at work.

Repentance and earnest prayer, resulting from a burning passion for the things of God, will bring forth a mighty awakening in the midst of this sinful mess our country is in. It is so easy for those who call themselves Christians to remain silent as the Lord's earth and everything in it is destroyed in the name of economic development. Blinded by the god of materialism which has given birth to greed, many now refer to God as "**my God**". They do not do this because they love and adore Him, but because they desire to possess Him so that He might bless their self-centered lifestyles. The term "my God" is now interpreted in the same way one would say my land, my house, and my shoes. Something else to own and control!

II Chronicles 7:14 turns this term "**my God**" upside down when it says, "**If my people**, who are called by my name, will humble themselves and pray and seek my face and turn from their wicked ways, then I will hear from heaven, and I will forgive their sin and will heal their land."

When God declares in this verse, "If My people," He is making it clear that **He is in control**. Now we must respond by humbling ourselves, praying, seeking the face of God, and turning from our wicked self-centered ways. Such action on our part, through the leading of the Holy Spirit and the redemptive work of Jesus Christ, results in God hearing from heaven, forgiving our sin, and making us the salt of the earth. This ultimately results in the healing of our land. Remember that "Religion that God our Father accepts as pure and faultless is this: to look after orphans and widows in their distress and to keep oneself form being polluted by the world" (James 1:27).

The time for action is now. May God heal us of our spiritual lack of saltiness and help us to be His church at this time of great need. We must indeed earnestly pray and strive to hear the groaning of creation and the cries of the hurting and homeless. Then by faith we must reach out to those in need through the love of our Jesus Christ. The time has come for us to pray and then practice true and perfect religion according to the Word of God and the leading of the His Spirit.

Chapter 5

Prayers For Justice Do Make A Difference

N ever before have I seen so many hurting people with so many needs.

Homeless families, women, and children like Kae who for three weeks was living in her car with her two children, homeless trying to get shelter through the city referral service. A few days before she found the help she needed at the New Life Evangelistic Center, she slept in an alley so her children might have room to sleep in the car. During the night she was raped in that alley as her children looked on.

A few miles away Rose was sleeping in the park with her two children, ages four and seven. As they slept, she was attacked and brutally raped in front of her children.

After Wilma's house burned down, she ended up on the streets and got sick. While struggling to survive she went to the hospital. Then the state took her children from her and put them into foster care.

This list of desperate cases goes on and on. **How do these people survive and what keeps them going**? Rose, Kate, and Wilma developed a ministry. This ministry confronted the injustice that was destroying their lives and their children's. Rose, Kate, and Wilma took their Bibles and implemented the secrets Paul revealed in 2 Corinthians 4. In verse 1 Paul says, "Therefore, since we have this ministry, as we received mercy, we do not lose heart."

We are not self-appointed or self-made men and women. We do not frequently choose what life thrust upon us, but out of it all, God forms and molds a special ministry for each of us. In each case the problems we have encountered always seem bigger than we are.

We know we are neither worthy nor able to achieve the task set before us. That is why Paul said in 2 Corinthians 3:5-6, "Our adequacy is from God, who also made us adequate as servants of a new covenant."

If you have committed your life to Jesus Christ becoming a recipient of the new covenant, then you have a ministry. At New Life Evangelistic Center, daily we are giving those who have a calling to serve God among the hurting and homeless the opportunity to fulfill that calling.

We must begin to hear the cries of the homeless and start to feel the intensity of their pain. Such an adjustment is not easy. After all, so much of our religion is an engagement in the pursuit of our own personal comfort and the elimination of pain in our own life. In such a climate of personalized religion it just does not make sense to try to hear and respond to the needs of others. Yet Jesus declares, "I tell you the truth, whatever you did for one of the least of these, you did for me" (Matthew 25:40).

As we desire to be guided by the spirit of truth, which Jesus speaks of in John 16:7-15, we begin to realize we cannot dwell in truth unless we effectively take sides with the unloved, the oppressed, and the downtrodden. To do such requires not only faith but the clear-cut directives found in 2 Peter 1:3-8.

"His divine power has given us everything we need for life and godliness through our knowledge of Him who called us by His own glory and goodness. Through these He has given us His very great and precious promises, so that through them you may participate in the divine nature and escape the corruption in the world caused by evil desires. For this very reason, make every effort to add to your faith goodness; and to goodness, knowledge; and to knowledge, self-control; and to self-control, perseverance; and to perseverance, godliness; and to godliness, brotherly kindness; and to brotherly kindness, love. For if you possess these qualities in increasing measure, they will keep you from being ineffective and unproductive in your knowledge of our Lord Jesus Christ."

If we are truly going to be effective and productive instruments of justice, we must first listen to the cries of the victims of injustice and then seek God for the wisdom to offer viable solutions. We are told in I Corinthians 2:9-13 the following, *"But, as it is written, 'What no eye has seen, nor ear heard, nor the heart of man conceived, what God has prepared for those who love Him,'"* God has revealed to us through the Spirit. For the Spirit searches everything, even the depths of God. For what person knows a man's thoughts of God except the Spirit of God. Now we have received not the spirit of the world, but the Spirit, which is from God, that we might understand the gifts bestowed on us by God. And we impart this in words not taught by human wisdom, but taught by the Spirit, interpreting truths to those who possess the Spirit.

In the midst of the cry for justice we must ask God for the revelation He provides through His Spirit. Sometimes He shows us direct solutions for the problem of suffering and issues of injustice. Other times it means standing in solidarity with those in need.

The questions of "where is justice," and "why me, Oh God," swirl around us. In complete desperation, often without clear direction, we are forced to our knees in prayer. Then as empty vessels God is free to first fill us with His peace, and then gives us the direction for meeting the needs God has shown us.

Sometimes such direction may not come for some time. That is why we must remain steadfast and pray daily for those in need. Psalm 82:3-4 tells us, "Defend the cause of the weak and fatherless;

maintain the rights of the poor and oppressed. Rescue the weak and needy; deliver them from the hand of the wicked."

Defending, rescuing, and delivering the weak, the fatherless, the poor and the oppressed also involve implementing the gift of hospitality. In Luke 14:13-14 Jesus commanded, "When you give a feast, invite the poor, the maimed, the lame, the blind, and you will be blessed because they cannot repay you."

Christine Pohl in her book, "Making Room" explains such hospitality. "God's guest list includes a disconcerting number of poor and broken people, those who bring little to any gathering except their need. The distinctive quality of Christian hospitality is that it offers a generous welcome to the "least" without concern for advantage or benefit to the host. Such hospitality reflects God's greater hospitality that welcomes the undeserving, provides the lonely with a home, and sets a banquet table for the hungry."

"Images of God as a gracious and generous host pervade the Biblical materials. God provides manna and quail daily in the wilderness for a hungry and often ungrateful people. God offers shelter in a hot and dry land, and refreshments through living water."

"Writers in the New Testament portray Jesus as a gracious host, welcoming children and prostitutes, tax collection and sinners into His presence. Such a welcome startled and annoyed those who viewed themselves as the preferred guests at gatherings. But Jesus, God incarnate, is also portrayed as a vulnerable guest and needy stranger, one who, "came to His own home" and often received no welcome (John 1:11). In His life on earth, Jesus experienced the vulnerability of the homeless infant, the child refugee, the adult with no place to lay His head, the despised convict."

"This intermingling of guest and host roles in the person of Jesus is part of what makes the story of hospitality so compelling for Christians. Jesus welcomes and needs welcome. Jesus requires that followers depend on and provide hospitality."

As we strive to be the hosts God has called us to be at New Life

Evangelistic Center, what our ministry needs more now than anything else is intercessory prayer warriors. The New Testament points out that there is a spiritual battle under way which requires each of us to put on the full armor of God (see Ephesians 6:10-18, 2 Timothy 2:1-5, 1 Timothy 6:12). Clothed in the full armor of God and equipped with the sword of the Spirit, which is the Word of God, we are then able to intercede in prayer. Then we provide the hospitality that Christ desires from His people.

Yes, these are trying times, times spoken of in the Scriptures that would take place prior to the return of Jesus Christ. He told us that at that time the love of many would grow cold as wars and rumors of wars, earthquakes and economic difficulties take place. At such a time like this it is critical that we know who Jesus is and what His resurrection means in our daily lives.

The risen Christ we are serving, as we feed the hungry and shelter the homeless "is the image of the invisible God, the first-born of all creation; for in Him all things were created, in heaven and on earth, visible and invisible, whether thrones or dominions or principalities or authorities – all things were created through Him and for Him. He is before all things, and in Him all things hold together" (Colossians 1:15-17).

It is because Jesus has demonstrated victory over death itself through His physical resurrection, we can be assured of the resurrection coming in the midst of injustice and oppression. We are told in Isaiah 32:3-8, "Then everyone who can see will be looking for God, and those who can hear will listen for His voice. Even the hotheads among them will be full of sense and understanding. Those who stammer in uncertainty will speak out plainly. In that day, ungodly fools will not be heroes. Wealthy cheaters will not be respected as outstanding citizens. Everyone will recognize ungodly fools for what they are. They spread lies about the Lord; they deprive the hungry of food and give no water to the thirsty. The smooth tricks of evil people will be exposed including all the lies they used to oppress the poor in the courts. But good people will be generous to others and will be blessed for all they do."

These good people are those who care about others and engage in **PUSH** prayers for justice. They are willing to do this until they see the promise of Isaiah 32:3-8 fulfilled. PUSH prayers involve **P**raying **U**ntil **S**omething **H**appens.

PUSH prayers are those prayers that are doing what Jesus told us to do in Matthew 7:7-8 when He said, "Keep on asking, and you will be given what you ask for. Keep on looking and you will find. Keep on knocking and the door will be opened. For everyone who asks receives. Everyone who seeks finds. And the door is opened to everyone who knocks."

Prayer birthed in the compassion of Jesus moves us among those in need, enabling us to experience that need in the depths of our souls. It causes us to obey our Lord's command when He says, "Ask the Lord of the harvest to send workers into His harvest field." Please pray for more NLEC workers to come forth. As we see the magnitude of need around us, let us cry out with the prophet, "My eyes fail from weeping, I am in torment within, my heart is poured out on the ground because my people are destroyed, because children and infants faint in the streets of the city" (Lamentations 2:11).

Compassion causes me to ask what would happen if I cared enough to wrestle with God like Jacob, if necessary, until my heart was broken over the pain of the hurting and homeless who have no place to sleep? As I hear story after story about the terrible things that are happening to the homeless, I find myself asking what would happen if I were prepared to engage in the spiritual warfare necessary, to see people set free from the cycle of homelessness.

The fact is you and your prayers do make a difference. The tragedy is so many are giving in to despondency, discouragement, disappointment, and depression. It is evident in their general "I don't care attitude." This is the result of a mistaken belief that what they are doing really does not make any difference.

In order for you to "always give yourselves fully to the work of the

Lord because you know that your labor in the Lord is not in vain," you must develop a healthy self-image as provided in the Word of God. Begin now to start seeing yourself the way God sees you. Remember, "The Lord is with you, O valiant warrior" (Judges 6:12). Yes, you may have made mistakes in the past, but thanks be to God, who through Jesus, provides forgiveness of sins and the hope of a new beginning.

We must begin praying now for justice and then "Run with endurance the race that is set before us, fixing our eyes on Jesus, the author and perfector of faith" (Hebrews 12:1-2).

This is no time to give up or give into the spirit of indifference to the needs of the poor and homeless. Instead, we must give God 100%, by earnestly praying for the homeless and then by doing our absolute best on every job He has given us. **Our efforts and prayers for good do make a difference. Our labor is not in vain.** At this hour, our Lord is telling us, "Have I not commanded you? Be strong and courageous! Do not tremble or be dismayed, for the Lord your God is with you wherever you go" (Joshua 1:9).

Chapter 6

God's Delay Is Not God's Denial

When God delays in answering my prayers it is easy for me to start believing He is denying me the resources I need at the moment. Isaiah 30:18 tells me that is not the case. "Therefore, the Lord will wait, that He may be gracious to you! And therefore, He will be exalted that He may have mercy on you. For the Lord is a God of justice; Blessed are those who wait for Him."

This verse explains why God waits. It tells me the needs are not immediately being met even though I may be naming it and claiming it done. God is waiting so He could be gracious to me.

I have wanted to respond by saying "Ok God, you can be gracious to me now with the $200,000 that the ministry needs to pay these bills, make repairs on the shelters and help all these poor and homeless people who are coming to us for help."

Even though the needs are very real and I have placed an itemized list of them at Philippians 4:19 in my Bible, God desires to show me He wants to be more in my life than just be my divine banker. **He desires to be exalted in my heart and mind to the point**

I know in the depths of my soul the extent of His mercy and justice.

Isaiah 30:19-21 goes on to say, "You shall weep no more. He will be very gracious to you at the sound of your cry; When He hears it, He will answer you. And though the Lord gives you the bread of adversity and the water of affliction, yet your teachers will not be moved into a corner anymore, but your eyes shall see your teachers. Your ears shall hear a word behind you saying, "This is the way walk in it. Whenever you turn to the right hand or whenever you turn to the left."

As I meditate on these verses, I am reminded **God's delay is not God's denial**. I must let His peace assure me of His presence to the point that anxiety will release its grip.

Along with the assurance that He is hearing my cries for help, the Holy Spirit also wants me to get quiet in my spirit so I can recognize the many teachers God sends to me daily to affirm His word and give me direction. "And though the Lord gives you the bread of adversity and the water of affliction, yet your teachers will not be moved into a corner anymore, but your eyes shall see your teachers. Your ears shall hear a word behind you saying, 'This is the way, walk in it,'" whenever you turn to the right hand or whenever you turn to the left" (verse 20-21).

Through these verses, the Holy Spirit is teaching me **to pray and not panic**. God's delay is not God's denial. He is trying to teach me to trust Him and seek His direction.

Jesus said in John 10:27, "My sheep hear my voice, and I know them, and they follow me." This verse is telling me to release all of my anxieties into the hands of the Father in order that the Holy Spirit can open my ears to the voice of Jesus. As I lay the financial needs of NLEC before Him I am then free to hear His voice and receive His direction when He says sell this, write this letter, send out this brochure describing the need, or wait, the gift you need is in the mail.

Waiting for the answer to prayer does not involve just sitting there doing nothing and expecting God to place the answer in my hands. It involves listening and seeking Him for direction day by day, moment by moment. "Your ears shall hear a word behind you, saying, this is the way, walk in it, whenever you turn to the right hand or whenever you turn to the left" (verse 21).

This word that is given is provided first and foremost in the scriptures. As I daily read the Bible and stay in touch with God through the power of the Holy Spirit it will be much easier for me to discern the voice of God from all the other voices.

While I continue to seek God I am reminded of David, who obeyed God and waited for God's will to unfold in his life. David was anointed, as a boy, to be king. From the time he was anointed to the time David actually became king, David found himself hiding from Saul and experiencing the anxieties, the injustices, and disappointments from being on the run. As this happened, David continued to trust and waited upon God as He sought His direction.

In Psalms 37:7-11 David explains why it is important to wait, "Be still in the presence of the Lord, and wait patiently for Him to act. Don't worry about evil people who prosper or fret about their wicked schemes. Stop being angry! Turn from your rage! Do not lose your temper – it only leads to harm. For the wicked will be destroyed, but those who trust in the Lord will possess the land. Soon the wicked will disappear. Though you look for them, they will be gone. The lowly will possess the land and will live in peace and prosperity."

David also shares in Psalm 37:34, "Wait on the Lord, and keep His way, and He shall exalt you to inherit the land; when the wicked are cut off, you shall see it."

The Holy Spirit is showing me that the reason David could wait and share this hope is because He knew that God is a God of compassion. "For the needy shall not always be forgotten, and the expectation and hope of the meek and the poor shall not perish forever" (Psalm 9:18).

When we feel forgotten, our expectations unmet and our hopes destroyed, we need to wait upon God to act and declare unto the

Lord, "**You are my hiding place and my shield; I hope in Your Word**" (Psalm 119:114).

The Word of God, commonly referred to as the Bible, could also be called the book of hope. In it we find the strength to wait. In the Bible the promises, power and presence of God is affirmed over and over. We are told to, "Trust in the Lord (commit yourself to Him, lean on Him, hope confidently in Him) forever; for the Lord God is an everlasting Rock (the Rock of Ages)" (Isaiah 26:4 Amplified Bible).

To trust in the Lord means to have faith in God. Faith is the substance of hope. As Hebrews 11:1 says, "Faith is the substance of things hoped for." It is this hope that God provides which gives us the ability to wait.

I have found such hope by also reading Isaiah 40. It is a fantastic chapter to study when you are facing overwhelming needs. Throughout that chapter over and over we are reminded that God is bigger than any problem we might be facing. We are told in Isaiah 40:8, "The grass withers, the flower fades, but the Word of God stands forever."

Throughout the rest of Isaiah chapter 40 we are reminded over and over what an awesome God we serve. He is bigger than every problem so why should we worry, for "It's He (God) who sits above the circle of the earth, and its inhabitants are like grasshoppers. Who stretches out the heavens like a curtain and spreads them out like a tent to dwell in" (Isaiah 40:22).

As the politician's rant and rave, and the developers try to run the homeless and hurting out of the downtown areas why should we fear? We can stand with those in need because verses 23 and 24 say, "He brings the princes to nothing: He makes the judges of the earth useless. Scarcely shall they be planted. Scarcely shall they be sown. Scarcely shall their stock take root in the earth when He will blow on them, and they will wither, and the whirlwind will take them away like stubble."

There is so much more in Isaiah 40 that reminds us that **God is bigger than every problem**. Isaiah 40 concludes by stressing how critical it is for us to wait on the Lord and have our strength renewed daily. "Have you not known? Have you not heard? The everlasting God, the Lord, the Creator of the ends of the earth neither faints nor is weary. His understanding is unsearchable. He gives power to the weak, and to those who have no might He increases strength. Even the youth shall faint and be weary, and the young men shall utterly fall, but those who wait on the Lord shall renew their strength. They shall mount up with wings like eagles. They shall run and not be weary. They shall walk and not faint."

We can wait on the Lord because God is in control and through Jesus Christ there is hope both now and for all eternity. **We have this hope because Christ is risen.** Now we are being taught to rest in that hope during this time of anxiety. "(Resting) in the hope of eternal life, (life) which the ever-truthful God who cannot deceive, promised before the world or the ages of time began" (Titus 1:2).

Paul refers to this as putting on the helmet of the hope of salvation in I Thessalonians 5:8, "Let us be sober and put on the breastplate of faith and love and for a helmet the hope of salvation." We have this hope of salvation because Jesus Christ paid the price for our sins by dying on the cross. His resurrection following His death clearly shows that as we trust in Him, we will be saved. "Through Him (Jesus) you believe in God, who raised Him from the dead and glorified Him, and so your faith and hope are in God" (I Peter 1:21).

As we are in God's waiting room, we must let Him do His perfect work in our lives. We must never forget that God's delays are not God's denials. He may have us waiting because we are not yet spiritually ready for what He desires to do through us. Also, we may be waiting because He desires to increase our faith. As the Scripture says, **"Those who wait upon the Lord shall renew their strength"** (Isaiah 40:31).

The trials, tribulations, and troubles we endure on a day-by-day basis can serve to build character and hope within us. This happens as we trust in our Risen Savior knowing that God's delays are not God's denials. "For our light, momentary affliction (this slight distress of the passing hour) is ever more and more abundantly preparing and producing and achieving for us an everlasting weight of glory (beyond all measure, excessively surpassing all comparisons and all calculations, a vast and transcendent glory and blessedness never to cease). Since we consider and look not to the things that are seen but to the things that are unseen; for the things that are visible are temporal (brief and fleeting), but the things that are invisible are deathless and everlasting" (2 Corinthians 4:17-18).

Because of God's infinite love, mercy, and grace we are people who can live in hope both now and for all eternity. Yes, there m**ay be financial pressures, but we are reminded that we are to "wait and hope for and expect the Lord; be brave and of good courage and let your heart be stout and enduring. Yes, wait for and hope for and expect the Lord"** (Psalm 27:14).

Chapter 7

Overcoming Obstacles Through Prayer

We do not need more teaching about prayer. What we need are people who will pray. The prayerless life is a sinful life. Samuel made this clear in 1 Samuel 12:23 when he told the people of Israel, "As for me, far be it from me that I should sin against the Lord by failing to pray for you."

As servants of the Living God, we must realize that we are not as believers powerless but tragically all too frequently prayerless.

What our cities, which are held captive by crime and inequality need more than anything else are intercessory prayer warriors. As the New Testament points out, there is a spiritual battle under way which requires each of us to put on the **full armor of God** (See Ephesians 6:10-18, II Timothy 2:1-5, I Timothy 6:12). Clothed in the full armor of God and equipped with the sword of the Spirit, which is the Word of God, we are then able to intercede in prayer, assured of victory.

This victorious intercession is possible because of the victory Jesus Christ has provided through His death and resurrection. It is for that reason we pray in His name for He has told us in John 14:12-14 the following: "I tell you the truth, anyone who has faith in Me will do what I have been doing. He will do even greater things than these because I am going to the Father. And I will do whatever you ask in My name, so that the Son may bring glory to the Father. You may ask Me for anything in My name, and I will do it."

God weeps when He sees the destruction that the lust for power has brought and the prayerlessness of His people. His heart is broken as He sees those He loves going into a Christ-less eternity because of the lack of prayer that the lost will be saved. God's love causes Him to weep among the homeless, the hungry and the hurting who are not prayed for and helped by many who claim to be Christians.

I cannot help but recall how over fifty-five years ago people began to intercede for a generation of youth who had fallen into the pits of drugs, sex, and despair. As they interceded in earnest prayer, the Jesus movement came forth and tens of thousands of young people turned to Jesus Christ. The same thing can happen today once we begin to intercede with the compassion that flows from the heart of Jesus.

When it comes to facing obstacles, prayer is absolutely essential. I could not have survived the last fifty-two years in the ministry God has given me if it had not been for prayer.

The disciples saw that in the life of Christ it was prayer that gave Him the strength to persevere. In Luke 11:1-13 we see Jesus teaching His disciples how to pray by first establishing the fact that through prayer they are talking to their Heavenly Father.

It is this knowledge we have a Father who cares about the obstacles we face that Jesus gave us the Lord's Prayer. In this prayer Jesus invites us to meet our Heavenly Father who is the one that Ephesians 3:20 says, "Is able to do exceedingly abundantly above all we ask or think."

In the Lord's Prayer Jesus not only introduces us to God the Father but He also answers profound questions relating to our priorities and identity as children of God.

Jesus tells us, **"When you pray say, "Father; hallowed be**

your name," by doing this He helps us discover our true identity as children of God.

The next declaration, "**Your Kingdom come**," states that as God's children our identity desires that His Kingdom comes, not ours (v. 3). When we seek first the Kingdom of God and His righteousness, we are promised that our needs will be met (Matthew 6:33).

"**Give us each day our daily bread**" (v. 3) is a prayer of faith that our Heavenly Father will provide for our daily needs. Not only are our daily needs met as we trust our Father in Heaven, but also forgiveness is provided as we forgive others. Jesus teaches this as He prays, "**Forgive us our sins, for we also forgive everyone who sins against us**" (v. 4).

It is then that as children we may ask our Father, "**lead us not into temptation**" or more obstacles than we can handle.

J.W. Acker in his book, "Teach Us to Pray" says, "The man (or woman) who truly prays this prayer is a person of power. When the Christian offers this prayer, Satan trembles when he sees the weakest Christian on his knees. Never was nor shall there be another prayer like it. Let us employ it fervently, profitable."

Following the giving of the Lord's prayer Jesus continues to teach us how to pray. He does this by showing us that our Heavenly Father is more dependable than a friend who reluctantly wakes up to give some bread when needed (vs. 5-8).

Luke 11:1-13 is filled not only with directions for praying but it also shows how our Heavenly Father is more reliable than an earthly father when it comes to giving good gifts. Jesus explains that our Father in Heaven gives to everyone who asks, seeks or knocks (v. 10). In addition to all these gifts, "**Your Father in Heaven gives the Holy Spirit to those who ask Him**" (v. 13).

As I get older, I continue to see that obstacles give me more and more opportunities to get to know my Father in Heaven better. Because of the great love He has shown me by sending His Son into the world to die for my sins, I have passed from death to life (John 5:24). Knowing this I can then pray when facing obstacles with

Romans 8:32 in mind. "He who did not spare His own Son, but gave Him up for us all – how will He not also, along with Him, graciously give us all things?"

As I pray, I become increasingly aware how much I am loved by Jesus (John 15:9), and my Father in heaven (John 16:27). With this awareness dwelling in me, I can believe what Jesus said in John 14:12-14 when He said, "Very truly I tell you, whoever believes in me will do the works I have been doing, and they will do even greater things than these, because I am going to the Father: And I will do whatever you ask in my name, so that the Father may be glorified in the Son. You may ask me for anything in my name, and I will do it."

I grabbed on to these verses in the early years of the ministry at New Life Evangelistic Center. As growing numbers of people were having their utilities shut off, I would go to my Heavenly Father and seek God in the name of Jesus. As a result, He had me approach the Utility companies with the idea for Dollar Help. This program is still being used by the gas company to encourage people to add $1 to their gas bills.

During the 1980 heat crisis, as a result of prayer, the Lord allowed NLEC for many years to distribute 1,000's of fans and hundreds of air conditioners to the poor and elderly.

Mike Bickle in his book, "Growing in Prayer" says, "Two of the primary requests Jesus exhorted us to make of the Father when we pray, are for the release of a greater measure of the Holy Spirit and the release of a greater measure of justice."

Bickle goes on to say in "Growing in Prayer," "that as believers under the new covenant, we already have the Holy Spirit. Therefore, we do not pray for the Lord to give us the Holy Spirit in the sense of the indwelling Spirit rather, we ask Him to release a greater measure of the Spirit in us and through us."

Instead of running from obstacles that would test our faith, we need to ask the Holy Spirit to show us how to apply Philippians 4:4-7, which says, "Rejoice in the Lord always. I will say it again: Rejoice! Let your gentleness be evident to all. The Lord is near: Do not be anxious about anything, but in every situation, by prayer and petition, with thanksgiving, present your requests to God. And the peace of God, which transcends all understanding, will guard your hearts and your minds in Christ Jesus."

I must confess that there have been times when I am facing an obstacle I am tempted to panic instead of praying. Panicking only creates more problems.

If I am praying and do not see an answer, I am often tempted to do 1 of 2 things. These include give up or try to run out ahead of God and solve the problem. Both of those options often lead to disastrous results.

In Luke 11:8 Jesus stresses the need for persistent prayer when it comes to overcoming obstacles. ***"I tell you, even though he will not get up and give him anything because he is his friend, yet because of his persistence he will get up and give him as much as he needs"*** (New American Standard 1995). Remember God's delay is not God's denial.

Perhaps you are facing an overwhelming obstacle. Then do not give up, in Exodus 20:20 Moses said to the people, "Do not be afraid: for God has come in order to test you and in order that the fear of Him may remain with you, so that you may not sin." Give it to your Heavenly Father in the name of Jesus. Jesus goes on and declares in verses 9-10 of Luke 11, "So I say to you: Ask and it will be given to you; seek and you will find; knock and the door will be opened to you. For everyone who asks receives; the one who seeks finds; and to the one who knocks, the door will be opened."

Two of the biggest obstacles I have faced during the last fifty-two years has been the ongoing financial needs and being patient since April 2017 following the closing of the 1411 Locust building. In order to overcome these obstacles, I had to pray and receive the daily power and direction of the Holy Spirit.

In Luke 11:11-13 Jesus stresses how critical it is that we pray for and receive the Holy Spirit. He says, "Which of you fathers, if your son asks for a fish, will give him a snake instead? Or if he asks for an egg, will he give him a scorpion? If you then, though you are evil, know how to give good gifts to your children, how much more will your Father in heaven give the Holy Spirit to those who ask him!"

It is the Holy Spirit that allows New Life Evangelistic Center to continue in spite of the growing financial needs. As we pray our Heavenly Father assures us He will provide at His perfect time. He has done this for 52 years and will continue to do such in the future.

One of the greatest things about praying is that it allows my relationship with my Heavenly Father and my Lord Jesus Christ to grow. It also helps me to see things from God's perspective.

Often, we think of prayer in terms of God meeting the need He sets before us. We face an obstacle, we pray, and then we expect it to be immediately removed. I have seen that happen over and over but then there have been those times when He has said wait.

I must confess after waiting almost 7 years to be able to fully utilize the 1411 Locust building to help the homeless, I am hating the waiting. **Yet it is prayer and the power of the Holy Spirit that enables me to do such.**

After praying and not seeing this building reopen to provide shelter, myself and the staff of New Life Evangelistic Center found ourselves following Jesus further and further into the lives of those who are living outside. There, not only have I found the homeless who are struggling to survive, but I have found Jesus in a new and powerful way.

Prayer not only helps us overcome the obstacles before us, but the obstacles in us when it comes to that deeper relationship Christ desires with each and every one of us.

It causes us to say in the depths of our soul, "**Father, hallowed be Your Name, Your Kingdom come**." Under the direction of the Holy Spirit as we pray, each obstacle becomes an opportunity for us to advance the Kingdom of God.

46

Chapter 8

Wake Up To The Power Of Prayer

The time has come for us to stop sleepwalking through life. We need to wake up and repent from our indifferences and powerlessness and start praying! Effective and powerful prayers are needed at this time because when God looks at our world, He weeps. He weeps because He loves this world. God weeps because the lust for power has blinded and corrupted the human spirit. As a result, instead of **gratitude** there is resentment, instead of **praise** there is criticism, instead of **forgiveness** there is revenge and instead of **healing** there is wounding. It is time that as members of the Body of Christ we wake up and pray because in our lives instead of **compassion** there is competition, instead of **cooperation** there is violence and instead of love there is fear, particularly when it comes to **helping** the homeless and hurting.

God weeps when He sees the destruction that the lust for power has brought and the prayerlessness of His people. His heart is broken as He sees those He loves going into a Christless eternity, because of the lack of prayer. God's love causes Him to weep among the homeless, the hungry and the hurting who are not prayed for. This happens as many who claim to be Christians, sleepwalk through life as they are indifferent to the needs of others.

I have a nephew who is highly intelligent and is often asked to speak at major conferences throughout the United States. When he was in New Orleans my nephew discovered he had a problem he did not know he had. He walked in his sleep. He discovered this at 3 am after getting out of bed at a major hotel and walking into the hallway. Wearing only his briefs my nephew woke up and discovered he had locked himself out of his room. He proceeded to beat on his hotel room door to no avail. His roommate would not wake up. Finally, he had no choice but to run down to the lobby in his underwear and ask the lady at the desk for a key to his room. Only then was he able to return to his bed and go back to sleep.

Even though my nephew's sleepwalking proved to be very embarrassing, it is even more tragic that so many continue to sleepwalk through life totally indifferent to the human suffering around them. It is a fact that God has called each of us to wake up and be prayer warriors. As prayer warriors, we will knock on the doors of heaven with the power and promises of scripture. Prayer provides the key to unlock an alternative future to one that often seems out of control.

Our prayer should be, "**Dear God, show us how to reach those who are hurting and do not know your love. Show us how to help them.**" Let us pray for the lost and lonely. May we pray for that innocent man who is the victim of a media lynching and now has a life in prison because of a set up. How we need to remember those who are hurting like the little child in that cold unheated home where mom's gas is shut off because her daddy ran off to leave mother with the kids. May the Holy Spirit lead us as to how we can share the love of Jesus Christ with those who do not know His love, grace and mercy.

Where are the people of God? Where are you when it comes to praying? Micah 6:8 declares, "*He has shown you, O man, what is good; and what does the Lord require of you but to do justly, to love mercy, and to walk humbly with*

your God?" No matter what problem our community may be having as we pray God will show us the answer. I have seen this happen over and over during the past 52 years. Through prayer I have witnessed Dollar Help come forth, Missouri Renewable Energy and many other programs come into existence that help the hurting, hungry and poor.

It is tragic so much time is wasted pursuing money and fame. This is time we could have spent praying and showing our love for God by reaching out to the poor, the fatherless, the widowed, the homeless and the hurting.

It is time to wake up - our stay on earth is temporary. Every day we live could be our last. How long are we going to laugh it off and sleep it off? Isn't our hope greater than our hangups?

It is time we wake up and pray until we can see that this country, which is in a pigpen surrounded by a church that too often is a playpen, can change. It is time to leave the prayer breakfasts for the battlefields of prayer. We have feasted long enough. Now is the time to fast and fight through intercessory prayer. We have clapped our hands too long enough. Now is the time to let those hands grasp the sharp 2-edged sword of God's word and fight those principalities and powers which hold the people of God in bondage or fear.

It took 10 plagues to shake Pharaoh's grip on Israel. What 10 plagues will it take to wake up God's people to the need for prayer at this hour? Time is running out —Liberties are drying up. We would be better off living six months with a heart aflame from prayer, devouring sin in high and low places, turning this nation back to God rather than die after 90 years loaded with theological degrees and every honor of man.

Preachers make pulpits famous through earnest prayer. Prophets make prisons famous through intercessory prayer. God knows we need a generation of prayer warriors who awakened, are burdened, bent, and broken under the vision of impending judgement and the doom of never-ending hell.

Today almost everything detestable in the scriptures has become morally acceptable. Right and wrong is determined by political correctness. May God awaken us and make us fearless prayer warriors who are too bold for the system to hold and too hard to be heard. Prayer warriors, who know in the depths of their being that the intercessor's prayer can change the course of history and see the miraculous unfold.

Intercession is defined as believing, persevering prayer where the intercessor identifies with the need, not only agonizing as a result of this need, but also going before the very throne of God and standing on the authority of the Risen Christ.

John Grisham in his book "The Innocent Man," tells the story of Ron Williamson who came within five days of being executed for a murder in Ada, Oklahoma he did not commit. Ron knew he was innocent but instead of praying he would stand at the door of his cell and scream all night, "I'm innocent, I'm innocent, I'm innocent." Then he would trash his cell. All this did was make his situation worse as it encouraged the guards and other inmates to further tease him.

Thank God Ron had two sisters who believed in the power of prayer. They would intercede for Ron hour after hour. As a result, through a miraculous chain of events Ron's life was not only spared but he was released from prison.

I often think of the futility of Ron's efforts when I feel like screaming in the midst of the injustices of life. Then I remember Ron's sisters and the promises of scripture, and instead of screaming out in frustration I go to God in intercessory prayer.

It is time for us to wake up and take the limits off God and realize there is a place where we come to the end of ourselves. Then God is free to move in our lives far beyond what we can ask or think. There is no limit to God's plan, purpose and promise for our lives.

Intercessory prayer under the direction and power of the Holy Spirit enables us to move into this limitless dimension. Through the power of intercessory prayer, provided through the resurrection of

Jesus Christ, we can be freed from all that entangles and frustrates our lives, and keeps us from reaching our full potential.

What our ministry needs more now than anything else is fearless intercessory prayer warriors. As the New Testament points out, there is a spiritual battle underway which requires each of us to put on the full armor of God (see Ephesians 6:10-18, II Timothy 2:1-5, 1 Timothy 6:12). Clothed in the full armor of God and equipped with the sword of the Spirit, which is the Word of God, we are then able to intercede in prayer, assured of victory.

The question is, are your knees dirty? Have you awakened up to the power and potential of prayer? Are you spending time in prayer? Prayer is communion with God. It acknowledges the ever-present reality of the Living God.

Prayer is a privilege that, as we engage in it, our relationship with God grows. Prayer is not an option, for we are commanded in the scriptures to pray. In I Thessalonians 5:17 we are told to, "Pray without ceasing." In Colossians 4:2 we are told to, "Devote yourself to prayer, being watchful and thankful."

In I Samuel 12:23 we see that prayerlessness is sin. As we study the Scriptures, we see that prayer is not vocalized worry. It consists of **adoration, communication, communion, confession, contrition, intercession, mediation, and petition, praying in the Spirit, submission, supplication, thanksgiving, travail, and worship**. Prayer is finite, sinful people coming into the presence of God. It is caring people waking up to the need for earnest prayer and then praying.

Jesus makes it clear that earnest intercessory prayer performs a vital role in destroying the citadels of injustice as He asks, "Will not God bring about justice for His chosen ones, who cry out to Him day and night? Will He keep putting them off? I tell you; He will see that they get justice, and quickly. However, when the Son of Man comes, will He find faith on the earth?" (Luke 18:6-8).

Prayer is not an alibi for indifference to the plight of the poor

(Isaiah 58:2, James 2:14-26). As we care for those God cares for, He will take care of our cares as we put our faith in Him.

How we need more men and women of faith like Epaphras who woke up and interceded, "Always wrestling in prayer for you, that you may stand firm in all the will of God, mature and fully assured" (Col. 4:12).

To wrestle in prayer means to engage in prayer in an agonizing way with an intense desire. New Testament believers awaken to the need for prayer, agonize in prayer with intense desires. The needs we are facing today are no less significant. Now is the time for us to wake up and pray.

Chapter 9

Reversed Thunder—Praying With Power

One of the greatest privileges we have as children of the Living God is to come to Him at any time in prayer. Prayer is such a powerful force in the universe it could be called reversed thunder.

George Herbert that great English poet from the past called our prayers on behalf of the poor, the fatherless, the widowed, the sick, hurting, and homeless reversed thunder. "Prayer is...reversed thunder, Christ-side-piercing spear, the six-days world transposing in an hour." Psalm 29:3 shares the heavenly powerful response to prayer. "The voice of the Lord is upon the waters; The God of glory thunders, the Lord over the mighty waters."

When believers pray, thunder resounds in heaven itself! Revelation 8:4-5 illustrates this fact. "The smoke of the incense, together with the prayers of God's people, went up before God from the angel's hand. Then the angel took the censer, filled it with fire from the altar, and hurled it on the earth; and there came peals of thunder, rumblings, flashes of lightning and an earthquake."

This scene in Revelation Chapter 8 reverses what usually happens with heaven making decisions that are acted out on earth.

The prayer warriors referred to as the saints have intervened. The uninterrupted flow of hopeless events has ceased. The unexpected has become suddenly possible because prayer warriors like you have prayed in faith. Two or three have agreed together. "Again, I tell you that if two of you on earth agree about anything you ask for, it will be done for you by my Father in heaven. For where two or three come together in My name, there am I with them" (Matthew 18:19-20).

History belongs to the prayer warriors who believe, agree, and stand on the promises of God. They are the people whose prayers produce thunder, voices, flashes of lightning and earthquakes that crack the status quo wide open. These prayers persevere for justice in spite of the obstacles. They know what is right according to Scripture and, as a result, will engage in prayer that brings forth actions of hope and help.

Prayer warriors know that prayer is never a private act. It is not vocalized worry. True prayer comes from the heart where a victory has resulted from an interior battlefield in which Christ now reigns supreme. In such a life, inner liberty results where the prayer warrior is free to act in obedience to God's Word and not the expectations of others. The status quo is rendered obsolete and the obedience to Christ reigns supreme.

If Jesus is not Lord, then all activity and activism only further enslaves us to the god of self. As a result, we will simply be caught up in self-centered passions and fail to discover the possibilities of believing prayer. Without a life immersed in prayer, our social activism and acts of charity will only result in self-justifying good works. Unless the rivers of living water, resulting from a relationship with the Divine, perpetuated by prayer without ceasing, unfold, the wells of love in our lives will run dry. As a result, we will take on the likeness of the beasts of self-centeredness that are destroying the wonders of God's creation.

Prayer in the life of the prayer warrior becomes the theater where one experiences the healing needed so he or she can battle the principalities and powers of this world. With the power of Christ flowing through them these prayer warriors pray with such a mighty power that the reversed thunder takes place.

They know true prayer is not just talking to God with their mouths, but it also involves the use of their ears and central nervous systems to hear and experience what God is desiring to say to them.

God created us to live in an interactive relationship with the Trinity. This relationship, made possible through Jesus Christ, enables us to be connected with God in every area of life. As a result, we must see prayer as something that involves every fiber of our being.

When we pray, we behold God's glory of creation with our eyes. We **hear** the wonders of His presence in the singing of the birds and **feel** His wind embrace us. We **breathe** prayer into our lungs with each breath of fresh air and thank God for it. As Saint Francis of Assisi wrote, "Hold back nothing of yourselves for yourselves, so that He who has given Himself totally to you may receive you totally." Every fiber of our being as prayer warriors belongs to God and communicates with God.

True prayer in the life of the prayer warrior involves the senses of the prayer warrior. When I go on my prayer walks, I love to pray using my senses of seeing and hearing, touching, smelling, and tasting. It adds so much more to praying than just speaking words. Such praying challenges me to further focus on God and the wonders of His creation.

As I pray, I want my ears to hear the birds and other sounds of creation. I smell the flowers and even taste a leaf or even a flower. Then as I pray, I touch a tree and the touch of the wind embraces me. My eyes are used to observe squirrels, deer, and other wildlife as well as the beauty of the flowers, tree leaves, sunsets and much more.

Praying with the senses causes me to praise God and rise above my troubling thoughts and see that God is bigger than every problem. Bonaventure wrote, "Concerning the mirror of things perceived through sensation, we can see God not only through them as through vestiges, but also in them, as

He is in them by His essence, power, and presence... We are led to contemplate God in all creatures which enter our mind through our bodily senses."

Prayer involves listening as much as it does speaking. It is also a call to "Taste and see that the Lord is good" (Psalm 34:8). Tasting and believing the goodness of God involves us as prayer warriors directly in the existential struggle against the belief that God is out to get us. Tasting the goodness of God confronts the lies of the enemy that God does not care and only rewards "good" people. Tasting the goodness of God in prayer involves being baptized in His grace and accepting Him at His Word when He says, "Come to me all you who are weary and burdened, and I will give you rest" (Matthew 11:28).

To pray with power means to breathe in the life of the Spirit of God by exhaling fear and unbelief and inhaling God's grace and goodness. The prayer warrior not only speaks, hears, tastes, and smells God's goodness in prayer, but, like the woman who was bleeding in Luke 8:43-48, touches the very hem of Jesus' garment. This touch involves grasping the impossible, knowing that with God all things are possible. Touching the hem of His garment means refusing to believe the lies and accusations of Satan and instead receive the promises of Scripture and make them our own. After all, as the very temple of the Holy Spirit, can we not grasp with certainty the pillars of His presence?

Prayer sharpens our vision. As we pray, God can open the eyes of our hearts to those things that really matter. On a recent prayer walk, God was speaking to me, showing me more and more of His wonders of creation. Then in His own still small voice He spoke to me how foolish it is to seek the things of the world when **all I need can be found in Him.**

In Christ we can see our true selves, and in His creation, we can witness His eternal power and divine nature. "For since the creation of the world, God's invisible qualities—His eternal power and divine nature—have been clearly seen, being understood from what has been made, so that people are without excuse" (Romans 1:20).

True prayer warriors are strengthened and empowered through the promises of Scripture. Martin Luther, who once said he had so much to do on a certain day that he had to pray for an extra hour, declared, "Our Lord God could not but hear me; I threw the sack down before His door. I rubbed God's ear with all His promises about hearing prayer." Jesus Himself reminds us that we are to hammer away in prayer until a breakthrough comes. [Luke 18:1-8; 11: 5-13]

Prayer is not only like thunder, lightning, and earthquakes, but it also challenges us to take new steps of faith in obedience to God's Word. Prayer is a new force field of power that when it is cut through by faith creates an electricity that propels us to new possibilities. As Karl Barth wrote, "Wherever we cast our eyes the dynamite is prepared and ready to explode. For impossibility is, as such, nigh at hand, ready at our elbow, possible. Impossibility presses upon us, breaks over us, is indeed already present. Impossibility is more possible than everything which we hold to be possible."

As prayer warriors let us pray for the victory of God over disease, greed, oppression, injustice, and death. Let us fix our prayers on the divine possibility available to our lives, community, and ministry. In the battles we encounter daily, let us never forget to put on the full armor of God as we take up the sword of the Word and the weapon of Prayer [Ephesians 6:10-20]. As Walter Wink writes, "When we pray, we are not sending a letter to a celestial White House where it is sorted among piles of others. We are engaging in an act of co-creation, in which one little sector of the universe rises up and becomes translucent, incandescent—a vibratory center of power that radiates the power of the universe."

Prayer gives you the strength to rise above your circumstances "by anointing you with the oil of joy" (Psalm 45:7). Praying with all your senses enables you to thank God and declare, "I thank you, O Lord, for the wonder of smell and ask that "my prayers will rise up to you as sweet incense" (Psalm 141:2). I thank you, O Lord, for the gift of taste for you feed me from your finest [Psalm 81:16]. I praise you my precious Jesus for the gift of touch and pray that I may come to know you in a very powerful personal way [Luke 24:39]. I thank you for the gift of vision, for I know that you dear Jesus are the light of the world, [John 8:12] and that you give sight to us in our blindness [Luke 4:18]. "Almighty God, I praise you for the gift of hearing; I know I am truly blessed when I hear your Word and keep it" [Luke 11:28].

"Rejoice always; pray without ceasing; in everything give thanks; for this is God's will for you in Christ Jesus" (I Thessalonians 5:16-18).

Peter Kreeft points out that, "We pray to obey God, not to play God. We pray to let God be God. Prayer is our obedience to God, even when it asks God for things for God has commanded us to ask [Matthew 7:7]. Prayer gives truth to our mind, goodness to our will, and beauty to our heart."

Developing a powerful prayer life, resulting in reversed thunder, where our prayers on earth cause powerful developments in heaven, is more caught than taught. In other words, instead of just getting more teachings on prayer, we must just start praying. As we pray faithfully and earnestly to our Father in Heaven in the name of Jesus, we will discover the value of PUSH prayers. PUSH prayers meaning praying until something happens.

With prayer comes a deeper relationship with the Holy Triune God. This deeper relationship is a result of the redemptive work of Jesus Christ. As we pray "without ceasing," we will discover God's delays are not God's denials.

ACTS of powerful praying are not vocalized worry. Instead, they are prayers ending up among the four living creatures and twenty-four elders, who take "a harp and they were holding golden bowls full of incense, which are the prayers of God's people. And they sang a new song, saying: You are worthy to take the scroll and to open its seals, because you were slain, and with your blood you

58

purchased for God persons from every tribe and language and people and nation. You have made them to be a kingdom and priests to serve our God, and they will reign on the earth" (Revelations 5:8-10).

The acronym ACTS spells out **A**doration, **C**onfession, **T**hanksgiving, and **S**upplication (asking). Such an approach to God in prayer, prepares us to enter the presence of God through Jesus Christ who cleanses us from all sin.

The Psalmist prayed, "May my prayer be set before you like incense, may the lifting up of your hands like the evening sacrifice" (Psalm 141:2).

In the presence of God our prayers fill the heavenly courts with a blessed fragrance providing the atmosphere of worship. These prayers are in turn "hurled to the earth; and there came peals of thunder, rumblings, flashes of lightning and an earthquake" (Revelation 8:5). Pray by faith, expect God's reverse thunder to take place in you and through you.

Chapter 10

Prayer and Effective Fasting

For 52 years now, every Wednesday I have found it necessary for me to skip my Wednesday noon meal and have special prayer with the New Life Evangelistic Center staff. We pray for the needs before us, and that God would work through NLEC and the Here's Help Network to witness many souls won to Christ. Prayer makes a big difference for Jesus Himself told us to pray in Matthew 9:37-38 for workers who will come forth at this time.

As I fast and pray, I am able to enter, in a small way, the world of the hungry multitudes who go for days without food. In Isaiah 58:6, God tells us what kind of fast He desires. "Is this not the fast which I choose to loosen the bonds of wickedness, to undo the bands of the yoke, and to let the oppressed go free, and break every yoke?"

What greater yoke is there than that of sin, and the damnation resulting from it. Every 24 hours over 150,000 human beings are swept into eternity in our world, and most are not ready to face the great throne of Judgment.

Jesus has come to set the captives of sin free both now and for all eternity. Should we not pray and fast for such?

As we pray, earnestly seeking God, the Holy Spirit will come upon us with such power we will freely share the gospel with the unsaved.

In Isaiah 58 we see in verses 7 through 9 that God's desire for us is to reach out through His love to the poor and homeless. Doing this, as we are fasting and praying, enables us to experience the Lord's promise of new spiritual power. We are told, "Is it not to divide your bread with the hungry, and bring the homeless poor into the house; when you see the naked, to cover him; And not to hide yourself from your own flesh? Then your light will break out like the dawn, and your recovery will speedily spring forth; and your righteousness will go before you; The glory of the Lord will be your rear guard. Then you will call, and the Lord will answer; you will cry for help, and He will say: Hear Am, I."

God has promised to answer and do a mighty work through each of us as we pray, fast, and reach out to those in need through the love of Jesus Christ. He promises to make us like a watered garden where we receive not only the water we need for refreshment, but we will also be a spring of water that does not fail.

In Isaiah 58:10-13 we read, if you spend yourselves on behalf of the hungry and satisfy the needs of the oppressed, then your light will rise in the darkness, and your night will become like the noonday. The Lord will guide you always; He will satisfy your needs in a sun-scorched land and will strengthen your frame. You will be like a well-watered garden, like a spring whose waters never fail. Your people will rebuild the ancient ruins and will raise up the age-old foundations you will be called Repairer of the Broken Walls, Restorer of Streets with Dwellings."

A Christian book of teachings that dates from around 150 AD entitled The Shepherd of Hermas states, "In the day which you fast, you will taste nothing but bread and water and having reckoned up the price of the dishes of that day which you intended to have eaten, you will give it to a widow, or an orphan, or to some person in want,

61

and thus you will exhibit humility of mind, so that the one who has received benefit from your humility may fill his own soul."

Augustine wrote, "Break your bread for those who are hungry, said Isaiah, do not believe that fasting suffices. Fasting chastises you, but it does not refresh the other. Your privations shall bear fruit if you give generously to another."

Augustine, a bishop in North Africa from 395 to 430 and author of Confessions went on to say, "Do you wish your prayer to fly toward God? Give it two wings fasting and almsgiving."

By almsgiving Augustine meant sharing with those in need. Fasting is our opportunity to identify with those who are hungry in a small way.

Isaiah 58 was very close to the heart of Jesus. You see this in His Words found in Luke 4:18 when He declares, "The Spirit of the Lord is upon Me, because He anointed Me to preach the gospel to the poor. He has sent Me to proclaim release to the captives, and recovery of sight to the blind, to set free those who are downtrodden."

Then in Matthew 25:35 He said, "I was hungry, and you gave Me something to eat; I was thirsty, and you gave Me drink; I was a stranger and you invited Me in; naked, and you clothed Me; I was sick, and you visited Me I was in prison, and you came to visit Me."

When Isaiah 58 says, "You will be like a well-watered garden, like a spring whose waters never fail," Jesus proclaimed in John 7:38, "He who believes in Me, as the Scriptures said, 'From his innermost being shall flow rivers of living water.'"

Why is it that if we pray, fast, help the poor, we still do not feel like a well-watered garden? Why haven't we experienced the promises and the victory stated earlier in Isaiah 58:9-13? That question was asked in verse 3 of that Chapter. "Why have we fasted and you (O' God) have not seen it? Why have we humbled ourselves, and you have not noticed?" God's response in verses 4-9 makes it clear that our relationship to our co-workers and others have a direct bearing on our relationship with God. The various forms of fasting including going without food, bowing the head like a reed, even putting on sack cloth and ashes, are all a waste of time if we continue to seek our own pleasure, drive hard our fellow workers, have a judgmental attitude, and are always irritable, contentious, and stirring up strife.

John Piper in his book, A Hunger for God, states that in Isaiah 58, "God is mercifully warning us against the danger of substituting religious disciplines for righteous living. No worship, no preaching, no singing, no praying, no fasting, however intense or beautiful—that leaves us harsh with our workers on Monday, or contentious with our spouses at home, or self-indulgent in other areas of our lives, or angry enough to hit somebody, is true, God-pleasing worship. Do not make a mistake here; true fasting may be a God-blessed means of overcoming harshness at work, and contentiousness at home, and self-indulgence and anger. But if fasting ever becomes a religious cloak for minimizing those things and letting them go on and on, then it becomes hypocrisy and offensive to God."

Piper goes on to say, "Woe to the fasting that leaves sin in our lives untouched. The only authentic fasting is fasting that includes a spiritual attack against our own sin. Is our fasting really a hunger for God? We test whether it is by evaluating whether we are hungering for our own holiness. To want God is to hate sin. For God is holy and we cannot love God and love sin. Fasting that is not aimed at starving sin while feasting on God is self-deluded. It is not really God that we hunger for in such fasting. The hunger of fasting is a hunger for God, and the test of that hunger is whether it includes a hunger for holiness."

True fasting is not a personal religious trip. It is a personal confrontation with a consumer-driven culture that puts our needs above those of others. Fasting is more than just going without food. It is the willingness to deny the continuous feeding of the artificially inflated appetites that drives us and tries to define our purpose for living. In other words, if sports, the attention of others, fishing, the internet, smoking, or anything else has become a driving force in our lives, then we need to recognize this obsession for what it is as we seek God to break the enslavement it has placed upon us. That is why God desires to introduce us to the freedom of self that comes from looking beyond our own needs to those of others. Jesus through His death and resurrection provides this freedom. Now He wants us to discover that ministry to the poor is not merely giving things, but a giving of ourselves. With that in mind, read Isaiah 58:6-14 and discover that God is calling us as we fast and pray not only to provide relief to those in need but also experience relationship with them.

Fasting and prayer is not a formula to advance our Kingdom, but that of Christ. When Isaiah 58:9 says, "Then you will call and the Lord will answer," it is saying that as we join the forces of love and reach out to those without food, shelter and clothing God will be right there in the midst of these territories of high-risk love, hearing our cries for help.

Now is the time for us to accept the fast that our Great Physician, the Lord, desires for us. If we are really hungry for God, and desire Him above all, the fast He directs us to be a part of in Isaiah 58 will truly fill us far beyond anything the world has to offer.

Chapter 11

Unlocking the Unlimited

rayer spoken by a person in realization of their impoverished conditions, when combined by faith in the resurrection power of Christ can move mountains. The fact is though, the poor and broken-hearted often feel so crushed by the problems they encounter in their daily struggle for survival, that even a simple prayer seems impossible to utter. It is for this reason that the ones who are sincere about helping those in need must know how to pray. Without prayer, efforts to assist can quickly degenerate into a paternalistic response, which then shifts into one of being cynical or even bitter. This happens when the person helping comes to the realization of their personal inability to meet all their needs.

It's not enough for the advocate of the poor to confront the politician, preacher, parishioner, person of business or anyone else with the problems of the homeless and the hurting. **True advocacy first involves taking the problems of those in need to God.** Such an approach to advocacy is becoming increasingly critical in a brave new world which once tolerating the poor and homeless now looks upon them with a growing amount of contempt. In this materialistic world, where the war on poverty is quickly becoming the war on the impoverished, the ability to pray can mean the difference between life and death. As politicians change directions according to the political winds of the moment, it is essential that attention be given to the direction provided in Psalms 146:3-9. There we are told not to put our trust in the politicians (princes) but in the Lord God, the creator of heaven and earth.

The fact is God cares. He really cares about the cause of the oppressed. He cares whether the hungry are fed, the prisoners are freed, the blind see or the downtrodden are lifted up. While others may give up helping those in need, God demonstrates His love through direct action. That is why Jesus, in His great teaching on prayer found in Luke 11, challenges us in verses 5-8 to be persistent advocates through prayer.

Jesus said, "Suppose one of you has a friend, and he goes to him at midnight and says, Friend, lend me three loaves of bread, because a friend of mine on a journey has come to me, and I have nothing to set before him. Then the one inside answers, 'Don't bother me. The door is already locked, and my children are with me in bed. I can't get up and give you anything.' I tell you, though he will not get up and give him the bread because he is his friend, yet because of the man's boldness he will get up and give him as much as he needs."

In this lesson on prayer, we see that we can approach God with the confidence that He is our friend. This is not only illustrated in that part of the verse which says, "Friend, lend me three loaves of bread," but in Hebrews 4:16 which declares, "Let us then approach the throne of grace with confidence, so that we may receive mercy and find grace to help us in our time of need" (NIV). The basis for such confidence is found in the two preceding verses (verse 14 and 15) which says, "Therefore, since we have a great high priest who has gone through the heavens, Jesus the Son of God, let us hold firmly to the faith we profess. For we do not have a high priest who is unable to sympathize with our weaknesses, but we have one who has been tempted in every way, just as we are – yet was without sin" (NIV).

In the same way as Jesus is able to sympathize with our weakness, even so, we must ask God to give us a heart for the poor. When this happens, we will begin to unlock the unlimited love of God which results in social change. Such compassion involves a love which seeks to help those who are hurting meet the needs they are facing. In the story found in Luke 11, verse 6, we see a caring man interceding with his friend on behalf of a person who needs food. He begs, "A friend of mine on a journey has come to me."

So far in this teaching on how to pray, we have seen illustrated, confidence in a friend who will help, and love for someone in need. The next step for unlocking the unlimited when it comes to helping those in need is a **description of the need**. In this case it involves having an unexpected guest with nothing to feed them. Notice the one interceding didn't say, "I'm sorry I don't have any food, goodbye. God bless you. I'll pray for you." No. He said, "Wait right here. I've got this friend who I know will help. I will be back with something to eat shortly." That takes faith. Such faith combined with compassion is something that is lacking in the lives of too many people who parade around with the name tag of Christian. These people are ready to give up as soon as the one inside answers, "Don't bother me. The door is already locked, and my children are with me in bed. I can't get up and give you anything."

Giving up does not unlock the unlimited when it comes to demonstrating a compelling love to see a hungry person fed. Such a love dictates that we **persevere by faith**, knowing that the God we are praying to cares about the needy and encourages such perseverance. The result is the need is met. "I tell you, though he will not get up and give him the bread because he is his friend, yet because of the man's boldness he will get up and give him as much as he needs" (Luke 11:8 NIV).

Jesus, in His teaching on prayer encourages each of us to unlock the unlimited as advocates before God on behalf of those in need. **Prayer is the key to the very heart of our compassionate God.** When that key is used by an intercessor who is a friend of the needy, the unlimited is unlocked. This is clearly illustrated in the Scriptures through the lives of great intercessors like Abraham, Moses, Samuel, Elijah, and many others. Their compassion illustrates that as we become a blessing to others, we can specifically count on the blessings of a loving God.

As we draw near to Father God through the new covenant relationship provided by our risen Lord and Savior, Jesus Christ, we discover that He is indeed a friend of the poor and destitute. Jesus is a true defender of the fatherless, the widowed and the oppressed. When we make this discovery through a study of the Scriptures, we are assured of the fact that we also can count on the love and compassion of God at our time of need.

The knowledge that God is close to the broken-hearted gives us the power to unlock the unlimited as we pray. Psalms 34:7 declares, "The righteous cry out, and the Lord hears them; he delivers them from all their trouble. The Lord is close to the broken hearted and saves those who are crushed in spirit. A righteous man may have many troubles, but the Lord delivers him from them all; he protects all his bones, not one of them will be broken" [NIV].

Over and over as I have worked with the poor and needy during the past 52 years, I have seen this promise fulfilled. At moments, I felt so crushed in spirit that I didn't even think I could get out of bed in the morning. The very people I would try to help would betray me. Others who I trusted would lie to me and steal from me. People in the community would level their accusations against me. But then at those moments when I felt completely destitute in spirit, I would find myself gripping that three stranded cord of unlocking the unlimited found in Luke 11:5-8.

That **cord** involves first recognizing that poor and hungry friend on the journey of life. These are the people who need help even more than I do. **Second**, realizing that God is telling me to be a caring friend to this person, I must be willing to take my eyes off my own problems and seek help for this friend in need. **Third**, I must always remember that the Lord is close to the "brokenhearted and saves those who are crushed in spirit" (Psalms 34:18). I can pray for others standing on the promise of this Scripture knowing as I pray, God is also working a miracle in my behalf and the personal needs I am facing will be met.

The fact is, I am not alone in my struggle, and neither are you. We are free to intercede for others because we know we have someone interceding on our behalf. Hebrews 7:24-26 says, "But because Jesus lives forever, He has permanent priesthood. Therefore, He can save completely those who come to God through Him, because He always lives to intercede for them. Such a high priest meets our need – one who is holy, blameless, pure, set apart from sinners, exalted above the heavens" [NIV].

Today as people find themselves encountering problems that were unthinkable just one generation ago, it becomes more imperative than ever that we can unlock the unlimited power of prayer. The nuclear family of the twenty-first century cannot survive without it. The epidemic of homelessness, drug addiction, alcoholism, teenage pregnancy, etc., should put all of us on our knees in earnest prayer every day of the week. Unless we are advocates before God, we are not only incapable of truly helping others, but we eventually won't be able to even help ourselves. What tragedy neglected prayer is, in the midst of so many needs and in the light of promises such as John 15:7, "**If you abide in Me and My words abide in you, you shall ask what you will, and it shall be done unto you**" [NKJV].

It was the words of Jesus, combined with His witness of love which unlocked the unlimited in the lives of the people He met. The strength and power of His word waits to be unlocked in our lives once we quiet the inner voices which scream within us. These inner voices of depression and revenge pull us in a hundred different directions at once. As this happens, we are totally immobilized as we are thrown in slimy pits of despair where at best, we shadow box with vindictive hearts.

Those who never learn to put on the mind of Christ, by hearing and responding to His voice, travel through life alone! As a result, they lead broken, disenfranchised lives. Putting on the mind of Christ in a world of social injustice involves first receiving Jesus Christ as Lord and Savior, and then daily bathing one's memories in the conscious love of Christ. This involves slowly walking with Jesus back through the wounded areas of our lives, stopping at each wound and letting His healing power of forgiveness be extended towards the one who inflicted such a wound.

Jesus' healing power will allow us to unlock the unlimited with the same courage that caused Paul to declare, "I can do all things through Christ Jesus who strengthens me" (Philippians 4:13) [NKJV].

Unlocking the unlimited power of God involves understanding that Christ's compassion was a prophetic compassion, which was concerned with the social and theological causes of suffering.

Jesus refused to put bandages on social cancers and use His unlimited power to advance Himself. He went straight for the cause and unlocked the unlimited. How many in the church have drifted so far from their Biblical and historical heritage that they feel such action is too radical?

In John 5, we have the example of the man at the pool of Bethesda. That man had laid there crippled for 38 years. No one cared enough for him in those 38 years to help him into the pool. But Jesus was different. He cared and unlocked the unlimited healing power of God as He told the man to pick up his pallet and walk (John 5:9). At once, the man did.

It wasn't long, and everyone knew that Jesus had dared to break a Sabbath rule of not working. The establishment didn't care about that lame man being there for 38 years. They just wanted to get this "nuisance" Jesus.

It was not a mistake that Jesus asked this powerless man to pick up his bed and challenge the rules of an establishment that needed to be stirred up. This community had become a stagnant selfish society that was content to leave a crippled man lying on the side of the pool for 38 years. Jesus not only healed the man but asked him to break the Sabbath rule. As a result, the authorities decided that Jesus had to die, so they killed him, but this death did not eliminate Him. Instead, a resurrection followed and unlocked the unlimited opportunity for all of us to spend an eternity in the presence of God forever.

In a cemetery in Indiana, there is an old tombstone that reads: **"Pause, stranger, when you pass me by. As you are now, so once was I. As I am now, so you will be. So, prepare for death and follow me.**"

An unknown person, after reading these words on that tombstone, stopped and scratched this reply: "T**o follow you I'm not content, until I know which way you went**."

The fact is many people don't know where they are going now with their lives or where they will go when they die. Paul in 2 Corinthians 4 gives directions for unlocking the unlimited love of God both now and for all eternity. He says in verse 16, "Therefore we do not lose heart. Though outwardly we are wasting away, yet inwardly we are being renewed day by day. For our light and momentary troubles are achieving for us an eternal glory that far outweighs them all. So, we fix our eyes not on what is seen but on what is unseen. For what is seen is temporary, but what is unseen is eternal."

Even death itself is not something to be feared because through the resurrection of Jesus Christ, as 1 Corinthians 15:54-57 says, "Death has been swallowed up in victory. Where O death is your sting? The sting of death is sin, and the power of sin is the law. But thanks be to God! He gives us the victory through our Lord Jesus Christ."

This victory involves going to a place after we die where we will unlock the unlimited love of God as described in Philippians 3:20. "But our citizenship is in heaven. And we eagerly await a Savior from there, the Lord Jesus Christ, who by the power that enables Him to bring everything under His control, will transform our lowly bodies so that they will be like His glorious body."

It takes faith to unlock the unlimited love of God in our lives. Stepping out by faith is necessary to let His love flow through us into the lives of the hurting and homeless as well as stepping into Heaven after we die. The Bible tells us "Without **FAITH**, it is impossible to please Him; for he that cometh to God must believe that He is, and that He is a rewarder of them that diligently seek Him. **FAITH** is the substance of things hoped for, the **EVIDENCE** of things not seen. And we desire that every one of you...through **FAITH**, inherit the promises...And for this cause He (Christ) is the mediator of the New Testament, that by means of (His) death (on the cross at Calvary for our sins), they (the believers) which are called, might receive the promise of eternal inheritance (Heaven)" (Hebrews 11:6; 11:1; 6:11,12; 9:15) [KJV]

Faith in God sees the invisible, believes that which has been historically validated, and receives that which has been promised. Spelling out the word faith in our lives and unlocking the unlimited power of God involves: **F**-orsaking, **A**-ll, **I**, **T**-ake, **H**-im.

It is critical at this time we live lives of faith, forsaking all, and following Jesus. Today the people helping business is not a popular business. If you refuse to eat at the trough of the politicians, they will turn on you and consider you a nuisance. Other well to do people set on gentrification and running the poor out of their neighborhoods will attack you if you try to provide a shelter for the homeless. Sometimes even the very people you are trying to help will not appreciate your efforts. That's why it is so essential that you unlock the unlimited love of God daily through prayer and acts of faith demonstrated through works of compassion.

In 1 Corinthians 15:57,58, we are told, "Thanks be to our God! He gives us the victory through our Lord Jesus Christ. Therefore, stand firm. Let nothing move you. Always give yourselves fully to the work of the Lord, because you know that your labor in the Lord is not in vain." These words are especially true for that unsung hero who day by day is caring for someone in need. 1 Corinthians 15:58 says "Don't give up! Your labor is not in vain." Yes, you may be saying,

"Why bother to try? Why should I go on, I can't take it anymore." Remember, "...Stand firm. Let nothing move you. Always give yourself fully to the work of the Lord because you know that you labor is not in vain."

The very ones you may be trying to help may turn on you. Those you try to share the Gospel with may scorn you, but rather than becoming disillusioned, burned out or bitter, look towards heaven and let God unlock His limitless power within you. As this happens, you will experience the unlimited love of God unlocked in your life.

You may feel hard-pressed at this very moment, but with this all-surpassing power of the Holy Spirit, you will not be crushed. You may be perplexed, not understanding what is happening to you but you will not be living in despair. Yes, you may feel persecuted by a society that has forsaken God, but you will know you are not abandoned because the unlimited peace of Christ has been unlocked in your life. Even if you are struck down by life's circumstances, 2 Corinthians 4:7-12 testifies, you will not be destroyed. Now get up. Don't lay there feeling sorry for yourself. God wants to unlock His unlimited love and power in your life today.

At this very moment, Jesus is extending His healing hand towards you. He wants to heal you in those areas in your life in which you have been paralyzed when it comes to fully serving Him. He also wants to heal your eyes, so you can now by faith see the unlimited love God has for you both now and for all eternity.

Paul, in Ephesians 2:5-8 tells us of this unlimited love when he declares, "While we were spiritually dead in sins, God made us alive with Christ. (You have been saved by God's gracious love.) And God raised us from spiritual death and seated us in the heavenly world with Christ Jesus. God wanted to show the superior riches of His gracious love for all time. He did this by using Jesus to be kind to us. You have been saved by God's gracious love through faith." Now move forth by faith declaring **F**orsaking **A**ll **I** **T**ake **H**im and let Him unlock His unlimited love for all eternity in your life.

Chapter 12

Let Us Pray

I
t is the man or woman of prayer who can remain strong and be
at peace despite the adversities. He or she knows that God is in
control and that He answers prayer.

What a joy it is to pray. Brother Lawrence stated in his
work, The Practice of the Presence of God, "There is not in the world
a kind of life more sweet and delightful than that of a continual
conversation with God. Those only can comprehend it who practice
and experience it."

Prayer is simply talking to God. Let's do it now by praying.
"Some say, Lord you are unseeable, but I have seen you this day in
the light of the skies, in the green of the earth, in flowing waters. To
those who say You are untouchable I would say I have felt you this
day in the warmth of the sun, in the wildness of the wind, and in the
touch of another. In and beyond my senses, in taste, touch and sound,
your mystery has been made known. At the ending of the day, in the
darkness of the night, in and beyond my senses let me know your
presence, O God in the name of Jesus."

Pray, pray, and pray some more knowing that all of
creation is proclaiming the presence of God. "***The crash of your***

thunder was in the whirlwind, your lightning's lit up the world. Your path was through the mighty waters, yet your footprints were unseen" (Psalms 77:18-19).

Praying also involves being still and becoming aware of God's presence in a new way. It is hungering for a deeper relationship with the Almighty "As a deer longs for flowing streams, so my soul longs for you, O God" Ps 42:1. Remember prayer also involves listening to God as He speaks to us through the wonders of creation and His written word. "The mountains may depart, and the hills be removed, but my steadfast love shall not depart from you" (Is.54:10).

E.M. Bounds in his book, *The Necessity of Prayer*, states, "Prayer draws its very life from the Bible. It places its security on the firm ground of Scripture. Its very existence and character depend on revelation made by God to man in His holy Word. Prayer, in turn, exalts this same revelation and turns men (and women) toward that Word."

I know from personal experience that getting alone with God this way isn't easy. Thoughts like charging elephants running through the jungle go through my mind. I am reminded of things I should be doing and calls I should be making. The flesh screams but I know it is only in God I will find rest, power, and purpose. Being in the furnace of transformation isn't easy but it is even harder to go through life angry and frustrated.

While in the furnace of transformation and solitude after going through two tragic events in my life, I would enter a silence that enabled me to receive the direction of God that I needed. This involved reading the scriptures and letting Him speak that special word in what seemed like a hopeless situation. I remember when going on these prayer walks in the dead of winter God would tell me to hang on because just like spring was coming in a few months bringing new life to the trees even so my spring would be coming. **I can now testify to the fact that it did come.** I know from this and other personal experiences that going through the furnace of transforming solitude God used the experience to make me **better not bitter.**

75

Even though I can testify to the importance of solitude with a silence that enables me to receive the direction of God, there is still so much more I need to learn about praying with my heart. I must confess that much of my praying is done with the mind, where I bring a problem to God in prayer. When I don't see an answer right away, I then tend to get frustrated and even upset. That is why I must pray in such a way that by faith the needs are moved from my heart to the very heart of God.

As I pray from the heart, I must forgive those who come to my mind that have harmed me or disappointed me. Then I must surrender every thought to Jesus realizing that the prayer from the heart is that prayer that comes forth from the very depths of my being. Sometimes it involves a heavenly prayer language. *"In the same way, the Spirit helps us in our weakness. We do not know what we ought to pray for, but the Spirit himself intercedes for us through wordless groans. And he who searches our hearts knows the mind of the Spirit, because the Spirit intercedes for God's people in accordance with the will of God"* (Romans 8:26-27).

Isaac the Syrian describes prayer from the heart this way: "Try to enter the treasure chamber... that is within you and then you will discover the treasure chamber of heaven. For they are one and the same. If you succeed in entering one, you will see both. The ladder of this Kingdom is hidden inside of you, in your soul. If you wish your soul clean of sin you will see that there the rungs of the ladder which you may climb."

Now let us pray from the heart by surrendering to Him as II Corinthians 13:5 says, "Examine yourselves to see whether you are in the faith; test yourselves. Do you not realize that Christ Jesus is in you—unless, of course, you fail the test?" It is "the blood of Jesus, his Son, purifies us from all sin" (I John 1:7).

As we witness many in these last days falling away, betraying one another, and hating one another as described in Matthew 24:4-14, it is critical that we let Christ the hope of glory dwell with us. Henri

Nouwen goes on to state that "Solitude shows us the way to let our behavior be shaped not by the compulsions of the world but by our new mind, the mind of Christ. Silence prevents us from being suffocated by our wordy world and teaches us to speak the Word of God. Finally, unceasing prayer gives solitude and silence their real meaning. In unceasing prayer, we descend with the mind into the heart. Thus, we enter through our heart into the heart of God, who embraces all of history with His eternally creative and recreative love. But does not this spirituality close our eyes to the cruel realities of our time? No. On the contrary, solitude, silence and prayer allow us to save ourselves and others from the shipwreck of our self-destructive society. The temptation is to go mad with those who are mad and to go around yelling and screaming, telling everyone where to go, what to do, and how to behave. The temptation is to become so involved in the agonies and ecstasies of the last days that we will drown together with those we are trying to save."

For this reason, it is critical that we fulfill the mandate of I Thessalonians 5:17, "**to pray without ceasing**". It is pointed out throughout the New Testament there is a spiritual battle under way which requires each of us to put on the full armor of God [See Ephesians 6:10-18, 2 Timothy 2:1-5, 1 Timothy 6:12]. Clothed in the full armor of God and equipped with the sword of the Spirit, which is the Word of God, we are then able to intercede in prayer, assured of victory. This victorious prayer from our heart to the very heart of God is possible because of the victory Jesus Christ has provided through His death and resurrection. In fact, our only right to come to God is because of the atoning work of Jesus Christ. It is for that reason we pray in His name for He has told us in John 14:12-14 the following: "I tell you the truth, anyone who has faith in Me will do what I have been doing. He will do even greater things than these because I am going to the Father. And I will do whatever you ask in My name, so that the Son may bring glory to the Father. You may ask Me for anything in My name, and I will do it."

Yes, these are trying times...times spoken of in the Scriptures that would take place prior to the return of Jesus Christ. Wars and rumors of wars, earthquakes, economic difficulties, and turmoil in the Middle East, the list of current events that Scriptures speaks of is reported daily in the evening news.

How critical it is that we know who Jesus is and what His resurrection means in our daily lives: *"He is the image of the invisible God, the first-born of all creation; for in Him all things were created, in heaven and on earth, visible and invisible, whether thrones or dominions or principalities or authorities—all things were created through Him and for Him. He is before all things, and in Him all things hold together"* (Colossians 1:15-17).

Prayer birthed in the compassion of Jesus moves us among those in need, enabling us to experience that need in the depths of our souls. It causes us to obey our Lord's command when He says, "Ask the Lord of the harvest to send workers into His harvest field." Please pray for more NLEC workers to come forth.

As we see the magnitude of need around us, let us cry out with the prophet, "My eyes fail from weeping, I am in torment within, my heart is poured out on the ground because my people are destroyed, because children and infants faint in the streets of the city" (Lamentations 2:11). Compassion causes me to ask what would happen if I became desperate enough to wrestle with God like Jacob, if necessary, until my heart was broken over the pain of this generation of children and youth whom Satan has ravaged?

Now Jesus tells us to engage in prayer from our heart to the very heart of God and move forth in the victory that He has already provided through His death and resurrection. The reality of this enables us to be delivered from the pits of anger, despair, and hopelessness to the extent that we are free to praise God. "As they began to sing and praise, the Lord set ambushes against the (enemy), and they were defeated" (2 Chronicles 20:22). Thank God that He has given us the wonderful privilege of entering into the ministry of Jesus for "He always lives to intercede for them" (Hebrews 7:25).

As we engage in this dynamic ministry of prayer from the heart, we must ask the Lord to cleanse us of all sin. Psalm 139:23, 24 says, **"Search me, O God, and know my heart; test me and know my anxious thoughts. See if there is any offensive way in me and lead me in the way everlasting."**

We must accept the fact that we can't really pray effectively without the Holy Spirit's help for, **"The Spirit helps us in our weakness. We do not know what we ought to pray for."** (Romans 8:26) As we begin to pray in the power of the Spirit, we must aggressively come against Satan in the powerful name of Jesus and with the sword which is the word of God. In James 4:7 we are told, **"Submit yourselves, then, to God. Resist the devil, and he will flee from you."** (James 4:7)

When you are praying from the heart don't be surprised if your mind starts going in every direction with one anxious thought after another. As this happens don't panic or stop praying. Instead, remember Isaiah 26:3 which says, **"You (Oh Lord) will keep him (and her) in perfect peace whose mind is stayed upon You because (he or she) trusts in you."** With our minds at peace, trusting in the Lord, we are then able to pray with power as we intercede in the name of Jesus who, *"Having disarmed the powers and authorities, made a public spectacle of them, triumphing over them by the cross."* (Colossians 2:15) We can pray with the authority of Jesus knowing that through His work of redemption the powers and authorities have been disarmed. He has truly triumphed over them by His death on the cross and His resurrection from the dead.

As prayer warriors experiencing the victorious work that Christ has done, we are told **"Do not be anxious about anything, but in everything by prayer and petition, with thanksgiving, present your requests to God. And the peace of God, which transcends all understanding will guard your hearts and your minds in Christ Jesus."** (Philippians 4:6,7)

Jesus makes it clear that earnest prayer from our heart to the very heart of God performs a vital role in destroying the citadels of injustice as He asks, *"Will not God bring about justice for His chosen ones, who cry out to Him day and night? Will He keep putting them off? I tell you; He will see that they get justice, and quickly. However, when the Son of Man comes, will He find faith on the earth?"* (Luke 18:6-8).

Prayer is not an alibi for indifference to the plight of the poor [Isaiah 58:2, James 2:14-26]. As we care for those God cares for, He will take care of our cares as we put our faith in Him. Faith is an essential element in prayer. Jesus, knowing the love of many will grow cold in the last days, asks, *"When the Son of Man comes, will He find faith on the earth?"*

Many today claim to believe God is everywhere while they live like He is nowhere. No wonder their prayer life is so powerless for, *"Without faith it is impossible to please God, because anyone who comes to Him must believe that He exists and that He rewards those who earnestly seek Him."* (Hebrews 11:6)

How we need more men and women like Epaphras who prayed from the heart and was *"always wrestling in prayer for you, that you may stand firm in all the will of God, mature and fully assured"* (Colossians 4:12). To wrestle in prayer means to engage in prayer from the heart in an agonizing way with an intense desire. New Testament believers not only devoted themselves to but also agonized in prayer with intense desires. The needs we are facing today are no less significant. As you pray earnestly know Christ is working powerfully in you.

Please continue to pray earnestly from your heart for New Life Evangelistic Center's financial needs, the NLEC staff and for the needs of the multitudes that come to us daily. **Let us believe God for a mighty outpouring of His Spirit!**

Chapter 13

The Acts of Prayer

I f we are truly going to understand the dynamics of prayer as outlined in the scriptures, we must first look at what prayer is not. **It is not vocalized worry or insincere speech.** To the malcontents who want God to mollycoddle them by ritualistically and habitually going to Him day after day with their empty talk and other nonsense that they call prayer, God says, *"When you spread out your hands, I will hide My eyes from you; even thought you make many prayers, I will not hear. Your hands are full of blood. Wash yourselves, make yourselves clean; put away the evil of your doings from before My eyes. Cease to do evil, learn to do good; Seek Justice, rebuke the oppressor; defend the fatherless, plead for the widow'* (Isaiah 1:15-17)

The God who has given us the miraculous gift of prayer is also a Holy God who cannot tolerate the offensive, foul odor of sin. Our sins arouse such a disgust with our Holy God that when we pray, He must hide His eyes from us. The hope for engaging in a prayerful relationship with the Almighty exists not in our good works or futile moralistic attempts, but in the Resurrected Christ. By paying the price for our sins on the cross provide the redemption we needed to regain God's favor. For that reason we pray in the name of Jesus who said, *"I tell you the truth, whoever believes in me, the works that I do he will do also; even greater works because I am going to the Father. Whatever you ask the Father in my name, I will do it in order that the Father may be glorified in the Son. If you ask anything in My name, I will do it"* (John 14:12-14).

The question is—how can our prayers be effective and productive? Remember, time in prayer is not just one begging session after another. It is an upward, inner, and outer experience. To help me remember that when I pray, I like to have my prayers proceed so that my prayer session spells out the word ACTS. First I engage in the A with stands for Adoration. This leads me to the C for a time of confession, followed by the T for Thanksgiving, and finally the S for Supplication or asking.

Often when I begin to pray until something happens, I am facing a need that seems almost overwhelming. In order to get my mind readjusted, I must first engage the reverse thunder spoken of in Revelations 8:4-5. When I **adore** God as the Psalmists do, I experience the dynamics of prayer to the extent my inner man is emptied of the anxiety, stress and pressure that tries to dominate me. The peace of Jesus that passes all understanding begins to sweep over me and I am strengthened with might through His Spirit in the inner man (Ephesians 3:16). Where there was tension and fear, "the eyes of my understanding" start becoming "enlightened" to the extent that I "... ***know what is the hope of His calling, what are the riches of the glory of His inheritance in the saints, and what I the exceeding greatness of His power...which He worked in Christ when He raised Him from the dead and seated Him at His right hand in the heavenly places"*** (Ephesians 1:18-20).

While I am engaging in the **adoration** phase of prayer, I am awakened to the reality of the awesome love of God. As this happens, I join Isaiah before the throne of God and hear the seraphim crying out, *"Holy, holy, holy is the Lord of hosts; the whole earth I full of His* *glory"* (Isaiah 6:1-3. Then when my inner being is filled with the presence of God, I must like Isaiah **confess** my sin. *"Woe is me, for I am undone! Because I am a man of unclean lips, and I dwell in the midst of a people of unclean lips: for my eyes have seen the King, th Lord of hosts"* (Isaiah 6:5)

The act of confessing is the C in the word ACTS. As I confess my sin a need for a Savior, the Holy Spirit is then free to do His work within me when I pray. For example, perhaps my wife does something that troubles me. If I run straight to God with the supplication, or request, rather than first the Act of adoration, confession, or Thanksgiving, I may miss something He wants to show me.

As I am engaging in the **adoration** stage of prayer, I am focusing on the goodness and grace of God. It is then the Holy Spirit often shows me that it is something I may have said for done that caused my wife to react the way she did. When the Holy Spirit shows me this, and I **confess** my wrongdoing and start **thanking** God for my wife, then I am free to pray more for her in **supplication** stage from a heart of love. 1 Peter 3:7 tells husband that the way we treat our wives affects our prayers. ***"Husband, likewise, dwell with them with understanding, giving honor to the wife as to the weaker vessel, and as being heirs together of the grace of life, that our prayers may not be hindered."***

My prayers can also be hindered when I let doubt and unbelief cause me to question it when Jesus says, *"Ask and it will be given to you, seek and you will find; knock, and it will be opened to you. For everyone who asks receives, and he who seeks finds, and to him who knocks it will be opened"* (Matthew 7:7-8)

Praying with adoration leading to confession and followed by thanksgiving builds faith as we go to God in prayer. Jesus tells us that it is faith that will move mountains of need. *"I say to you, if you have faith as a mustard seed, you will say to this mountain, 'move from here to there', it will move; and nothing will be impossible for you"* (Matthew 17:20)

Adoration and **thanksgiving** are both upward bound, which is absolutely essential when it come to understanding the dynamics of prayer. **The more we focus upward on the greatness of God the smaller the mountain of need we are facing will seem**. Skipping the upward bound focus of adoration and thanksgiving and going straight to the outward-bound focus of supplication only magnifies the problem. This often results in our prayers becoming vocalized worry sessions over what seems like impossible needs, rather than upward relational communication with the Lord of Lords and King of Kings.

The stress resulting from the pressure of the need, pressing in from every direction, can make it difficult to have an attitude of gratitude. Yet it is this attitude of **thanksgiving** which paves the way for faith to be released. To be Abe to thank God when the pressing need is still evident, requires us to truly believe that God is bigger than every problem and can truly meet every need.

Romans 10:17 tells us that *"...faith come by hearing, and hearing by the word of God."* As we proceed to pray in **adoration** unto God, followed by **confessing** our need for Him and **thanking** Him for all He has done, our hearts and minds are opened to receive God's word and the seeds of faith are planted. It is then we are able to cry out with David, *"Hear my prayer O Lord. Give ear to my **supplications**! In Your faithfulness, answer me, and in Your righteousness deliver me. For the enemy has persecuted my soul; he has crushed my life to the ground; he has made me dwell in the darkness like those who have long been dead. Therefore, my spirit is overwhelmed within me; my heart within me is distressed"* (Psalm 143:1, 3-4).

I must confess there are those times when one battle after another takes place. I feel my spirit overwhelmed within me and my heart is distressed. At times like that I don't even feel like praying, but I know God's word tells me I can't give up. Instead, I have to engage in the dynamics of prayer like David did in verses 5 and 6 of Psalm 143.

1. David says, *"**I remember the days of old.**"* When I feel overwhelmed by pressures and attacks both from within and without, I must bring to remembrance the miracles I have seen take place

during the last fifty-two years at New Life Evangelistic Center. As I remember how God has miraculously provided in the past, I find strength to face the needs of the present and the uncertainty of the future.

2. David says *"I meditate on all your works; I muse on the work of your hands."* David was strengthened and experienced the dynamics of prayer when He looked around and meditated on all the wonders of God's creation (see Psalm 104). Not only can we go on a prayer walk and meditate on all of God's works of creation, but we also have two things that David didn't have. These include the written word of the Bible and the redemptive work of Christ's death and resurrection.

Meditating daily on God's works and words, fills us with the faith needed to take the needs of the hurting, homeless and hungry to the throne of grace and declare with David, *"I spread out my hands to You"* (Psalms 143:6) in prayer. In Hebrews 4:16 we are told, *"Let us come boldly to the throne of grace that we may obtain mercy and find grace to help in time of need."*

The miracle of prayer involves the prayer of **ACTS**. It results in acts of faith and compassion. The adoration and thanksgiving phases involve prayer that are upward bound. Those that result in confession are inward bound and prayers of supplication, or requesting that a certain need would be met, are outward bound.

True prayer involves both the making of requests and the development of a relationship with God. David expresses this desire to draw closer to God when He cries out to God at the end of verse 6 of Psalm 143, *"My soul longs for you like a thirsty land."* It is the desire for God that delivers us from the slavery of sin and the lusts of the world. Paul tells us, *"If then you were raised with Christ, seek those things which are above, where Christ is, sitting at the right hand of God. Set your mind on things above, not on things on the earth. For you died, and your life is hidden with Christ in God. When Christ, who is our life appears, then you also will appear with Him in glory*" (Colossians 3:1-4).

Seeking those things that are above is not an invitation to be so heavenly minded that we are of no earthly good. It is a challenge to those who are always talking about what they are going to do for the kingdom of God, but never doing it, to be filled with the mind of Christ and the power of the Holy Spirit. When this happens to a believer, they earnestly pray and work until they turn their world through the power of the Holy Spirit upside down for the glory of God. As a result the hungry are fed, the homeless housed, the thirsty given drink, the naked clothed and the sick and imprisoned are visited as explained in Matthew 25:31-46.

As this revolution of love comes forth in word and deed, Isaiah 1:17 will flow from the life of the prayer warrior. These believers who have a relationship with the living God, through the resurrection power of Jesus, are told to "...*learn to do goo; seek justice, rebuke the oppressor; defend the fatherless, plead for the widow*."

ACTS of prayer are urgently needed for the work of New Life Evangelistic Center. Now NLEC is engaged in a major battle to provide shelter for the fatherless, widowed, homeless veterans and others in need. As New Life seeks justice and rebukes the oppressor, the principalities, and powers of the evil one attack day after day. The staff of New Life Evangelistic Center are declaring by faith and the word of God, "*The Lord is on my side; I will not fear. What can man do to me?* (Psalm 118:6)

The ACTS of prayer assure us as we pray that, "*He shall regard the prayer of the destitute, and shall not despise their prayer*" (Psalm 102:17)

We must now pray that revival will come forth, where those who say they are followers of Jesus Christ will be healed from the spiritual disease of indifference toward those who are hurting , hungry, and homeless. The time has come for the ACTS of prayer to come forth as we declare, "*For great is the glory of the Lord though the Lord is* high, yet He regards the lowly; but the proud He knows from afar. Though I walk in the midst of trouble, you will revive me; you will stretch out your hand against the wrath of my enemies, and your right hand will save me. The Lord will perfect that which concerns me; your mercy, O Lord, endures forever. Do not forsake the works of Your hands" (Psalm 138:5-8).

Resolve now to engage every morning and evening as the Spirit directs throughout the day in ACTS of prayer. Start out with **Adoration**, **Confession**, **Thanksgiving** and **Supplication** and then go forth by faith and perform the acts of compassion that are so urgent at this moment of history. As you do this, may God bless you **in a very special way.**

I want to invite you to join the New Life Evangelistic Center staff and partners as we pray and serve our Risen Lord and Savior Jesus Christ.

Join us by downloading the NLEC TV App on your smart device. With the NLEC TV App you will find free wholesome family television and inspirational radio. In addition, there is 24-hour streaming of creation messages and videos. You can also watch classic movies, inspirational messages, Here's Help shows to connect you with the poor and homeless, and much more!

You can also stay connected with NLEC via the following online social media platforms.

Facebook @NewLifeStL

Twitter @NewLifeStL

Instagram @NewLifeStL

Pinterest @contactNLEC

YouTube @NewLifeEvangelistiCenterOrg

And at our Website:

ww.nlecstl.org OR www.newlifeevangelisticcenter.org

Made in the USA
Monee, IL
18 February 2024

53139343R00059